GETTING THE BEST FROM

CLAY GARDENS

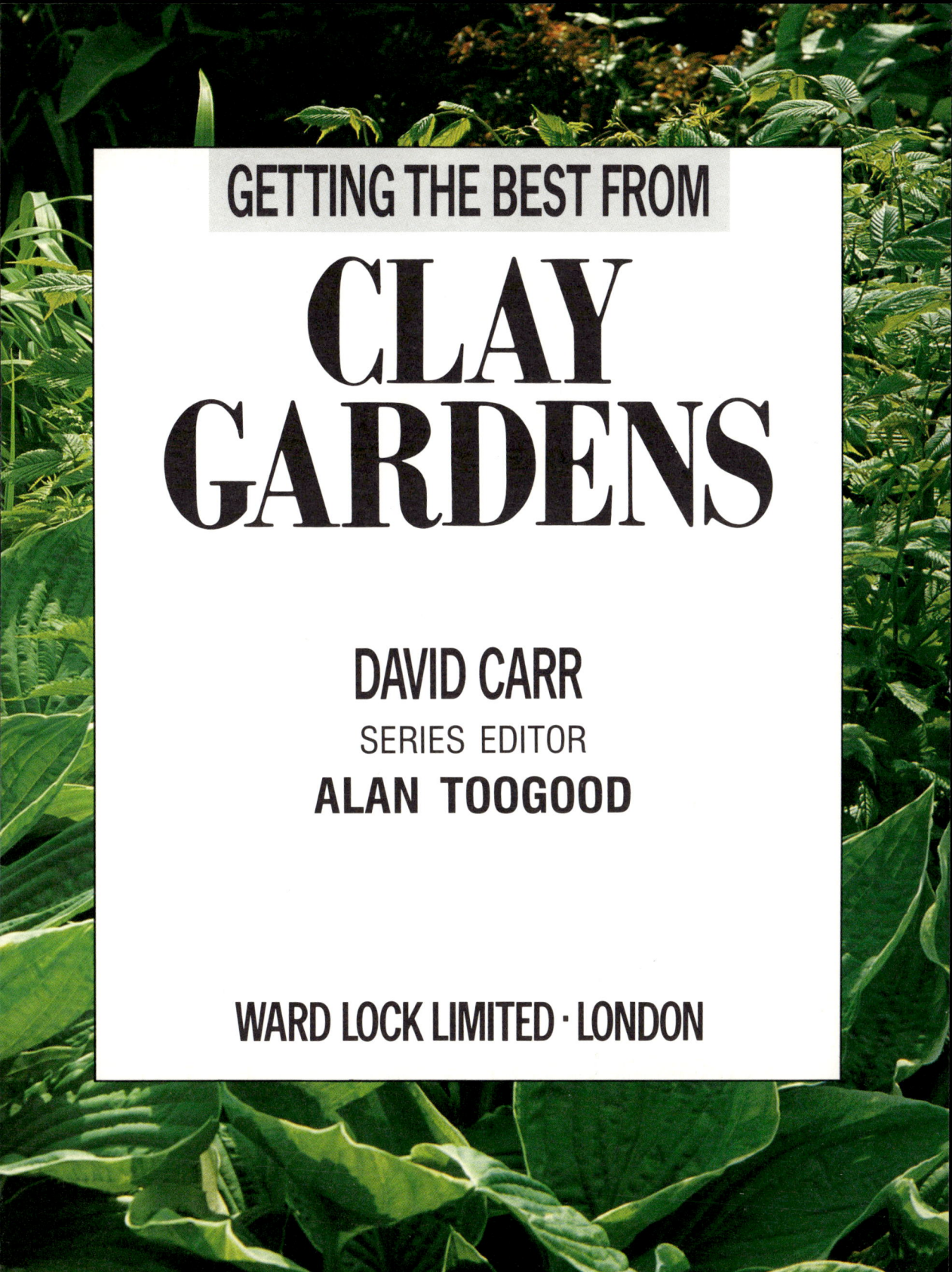

GETTING THE BEST FROM

CLAY GARDENS

DAVID CARR

SERIES EDITOR

ALAN TOOGOOD

WARD LOCK LIMITED · LONDON

First published in Great Britain in 1989 by Ward Lock Limited, 8 Clifford Street London W1X 1RB, an Egmont Company.

Designed by David Robinson

Typeset by Jamesway Graphics Hanson Close Middleton Manchester M24 2HD

Printed and bound by Rotolito, Milan, Italy.

British Library Cataloguing in Publication Data

Carr, David, 1930–
  Getting the best from gardening on clay.
  1. Gardens with alkaline soils & gardens with clay soils. Plants. Cultivation
  I. Title
  635.9'55

ISBN 0-7063-6759-6

Previous Page:
Foliage gardens can be outstanding and are good for shady spots. Here feathery ferns, fronted by bold hostas grow in harmony offering a contrast of texture.

Cover: *The range of plants that can be grown in clay soil is extremely large, especially if soil drainage can be improved. Seen here is a collection of dwarf conifers and hardy perennials, including orange crocosmia found at Tatton Park, Knutsford, Cheshire.*

CONTENTS

INTRODUCTION

The old adage 'clay soil is a man's soil – and sandy soil is for boys' is as true today as it ever was. It also accurately sets the scene as to what is entailed when gardening on clay. Initially a lot of hard work is called for. Until its physical condition has been improved, newly broken-in clay soil is heavy to handle by any standards. Spreading and digging in generous applications of bulky organics and conditioners, for instance, is vital in the early days. Thereafter, provided it is managed correctly, clay soil is fertile and highly nutritious with the heaviest yielding potential of all soils. However, it is also fair to say that success is more dependent on the effort, know how and attention to detail by the individual concerned than when dealing with any other type of soil.

Understand clay soil and the rewards are enormous. And that is what this book is all about – making the best of clay soil. The provision of shelter comes under discussion – a very important matter when gardening on clay. Likely drainage problems are high-lighted and ways of improving the situation outlined.

The whole question of plant varieties is brought into focus. For example, the wisdom of selecting quick maturing varieties. These are better suited to the relatively short growing season associated with clay soils which are slow to warm up in spring. Also discussed is the need to avoid over vigorous kinds which inevitably make excessive growth when planted in fertile, moist clay soils. By a similar token, the advisability of opting for dwarfing rootstocks wherever possible is underlined as is the need to give priority to the timing of operations — a facet of clay gardening which cannot be too firmly stressed.

The book goes on to pinpoint the wide range of plants suited to clay gardens. Included are shrubs, conifers, climbers, hardy perennials, bulbs, alpine and rock plants – as well as vegetables and herbs. Brief details of each are given and their compatability with the local climate. This is very important when growing plants on clay soils.

Waterside plants are a traditional feature of clay soil gardens. A summer scene where pink and white astilbes in bloom are offset with mixed foliage.

SOIL CHART

Colts foot

How do I know I have clay soil?

Ask the following questions:

Q What can be learnt from the soil?

A *The smear and plastic ring tests.* These are pretty reliable guides and do not require the need for laboratory testing. First, rub a pinch of wet soil between finger and thumb. Clay soil will leave a glazed smear and feel greasy to the touch.

The ring test is fully described on page 13. In essence, if a finger of damp soil can be bent round to form a circle without breaking, the sample under scrutiny contains a high proportion of clay.

Stickiness   Clay soils become glutinous and stick to tools and feet when wet. When in this state, they are difficult or impossible to work with.

Ponding   Surface ponding does occur on clay soils. But a similar effect is likely on almost any type of soil which suffers from over compaction.

Shrinkage   On drying out in hot weather, clay soils shrink dramatically, leaving wide cracks or fissures – easily seen when walking over bare ground.

Q What weeds are growing in my garden?

A Weeds are not an infallible guide since they are influenced by climate, soil lime content and other factors including cultivations. However, here are a few which thrive particularly well on clay soils:

- Celandine *(Ranunculus ficaria)*
- Creeping buttercup *(Ranunculus repens)*

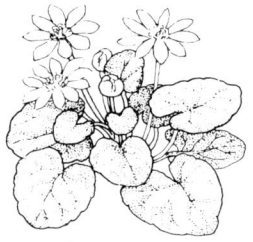

Creeping Buttercup

Celandine

- Colt's foot *(Tussilago farfara)*
- Rushes (juncus)
- Sedges (carex)

Q **Which plants are much in evidence and grow well in the immediate neighbourhood?**

A Researching these facts can provide some useful clues. But caution is needed when reading the signs. This is because soil type can change completely within very short distances. Also, the skill or otherwise of the gardener has a marked influence on the vegetation. Indicators of moist soil and probable clay are:

- Alder trees (alnus)
- Astilbes and meadow-sweet *(Filipendula ulmaria)*
- Hostas
- Primulas and roses
- Willows (salix)

Q **What is the local land form?**

A This can help, but only where the ground levels have not been completely altered by major construction works like motorways and new town developments. Moist clay soils are most likely to occur:

- In low lying, water collecting areas, surrounded by high ground.
- Near slow moving water courses.
- Near the lower reaches of rivers and estuaries
- On coastal, and inland, plains where there are natural glacial deposits. These are typical of the boulder clays of parts of Northumberland and Yorkshire, and around Bedfordshire and London.

Primula

Hostas

Astilbes

CLAY SOILS AND THEIR MERITS

KNOW YOUR SOIL

Clay soils have great potential for gardeners as in general they are naturally rich in plant nutrients. When well managed, they are highly fertile giving good quality of crops and yields which are normally better than on any other type of soil. Unfortunately, the reverse is also true: badly managed clay soils are difficult to cope with and can spell disaster. Anyone who has tried to work

Far left: *Double marsh marigolds are natives of heavy soils and ideal for a pool's edge. Note the yellow variegated iris foliage standing stiffly to their rear.*

Left: *Roses are often associated with heavy soils. Here a rambler rose is seen growing through* Buddleia alternifolia. *A daring idea for the larger garden.*

clay soils when they are too wet knows that it can be very difficult as it sets rock hard as it dries.

When taking over any garden, a determination to make the most of the soil available, goes a long way towards success. The first step is to find out all you can about the soil; the second is how to use this knowledge to maximum effect. These facts particularly apply to clay gardens.

PROPERTIES OF CLAY SOILS

Physical properties

As a quirk of nature, clay soils tend to be found where the land is low-lying or flat — ground which forms a natural collecting area for drainage waters from surrounding higher land. In many instances, this is one of the main reasons why they remain wet and boggy for such long periods.

One of the most notable features of clay soils is the change in physical condition as the moisture content varies. After prolonged rain, or irrigation, clay soils tend to become waterlogged with surface ponding. Drainage is notoriously sluggish and the drying out process is slow. While from a cultivation angle, wet clays will stick tenaciously to feet and tools. When clay soils dry out they become iron hard making cultivation almost impossible. Less immediately apparent is the fact that clay soils also expand considerably when wet and then shrink quite dramatically on drying to leave wide cracks. But even more important, this expansion and contraction also causes uneven settlement. This is of particular importance when planting trees in the vicinity of buildings, see page 21. On the positive side, the way in which clay soils expand and contract, coupled with their tendency to heave when frozen, can be exploited to good effect as a means of improving their structure. If they are dug up into ridges in autumn to expose a substantial surface area, and then left to alternate wetting, drying and freezing throughout winter, they are easier to work. Even the most obstinate clay soils stand a good chance of breaking down to a good crumbly tilth by the following spring.

All clay soils are slow to warm up in the spring, with the result that all crops are later to mature than on say sandy soils in the same locality. But a lot depends upon the soil's composition and its handling properties. Soils which are predominantly clay, but contain appreciable quantities of sand and/or organic matter come into the heavy loam category. Heavy loams are generally easier to cultivate and they drain more readily than the stiffer clays. The colour of clay soils often gives some indication as to their content. Heavy clay loams tend to be darker than stiff clays, ranging from browns to black if they contain appreciable amounts of organic matter. The darker the soil, the higher the organic matter content and the more fertile it is likely to be. Heavy soils which are whitish, or light coloured, pasty when wet, but hard and flinty when dry, almost certainly contain chalk, and are invariably neutral or alkaline. Clay soils which are stiff and yellow are short of organic matter. They are often acid and usually contain oxides or iron and aluminium. These soils need careful handling, but can be made highly fertile. However, unless they are limed, manured and cultivated they are likely to form hard impervious layers. Stiff blue clays are normally a sign that drainage is poor. If there is any suggestion of a rotting stench or bad eggs smell, you can expect prolonged periods of waterlogging. These soils are often on the acid side and need good drainage before planting.

Testing for clay content

A sample of moist clay is quite plastic-like in texture. It can be rolled out into long fingers which will bend round into a circle without breaking. Wet clay when squeezed between finger and thumb feels soft and greasy and leaves a shiny smear. If dry clay soil is crushed it will be seen to be composed of dust-like particles.

Fig. 1. Finding out what your soil is is the first step towards it's treatment.

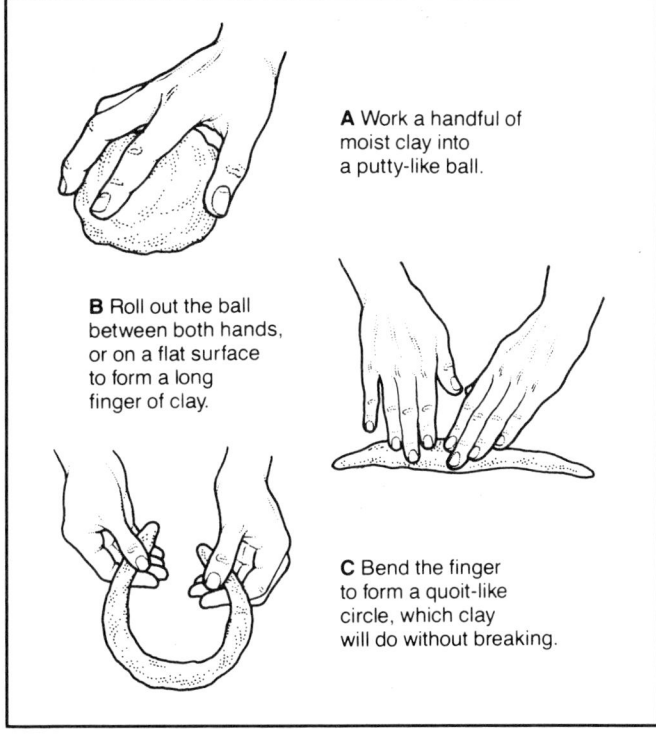

A Work a handful of moist clay into a putty-like ball.

B Roll out the ball between both hands, or on a flat surface to form a long finger of clay.

C Bend the finger to form a quoit-like circle, which clay will do without breaking.

Chemical properties

Clay soils possess a 'high buffer capacity.' This gives plants good protection from an excess or deficiency of minerals and nutrients. Over-zealous application of fertilizers or lime is less likely to harm plants on clay than on sandy soils. Any excess fertilizer is safely held in reserve. Clay soils are less likely to be extremely acid or extremely alkaline when compared to those which are naturally high in sand, peat or chalk. The buffer effect has other implications in connection with the use of selective weed-killers and liming. Garden plants which are particularly liable to weedkiller damage are marginally safer on clay than on sandy soils. Plants like young dogwood (cornus), euonymus, forsythia, hebe, honeysuckle (lonicera) and mock orange (philadelphus) will suffer badly if weedkillers are used in the near vicinity on sandy soils. And yet they will establish themselves without undue setback on clays. You will find that when it comes to liming, more generous applications will need to be given to clay soils than sandy in order to achieve the same degree of change. Weedkillers will also need to be applied in larger amounts.

Roses grow well in clay soils, provided they are well tended. Don't plant them unless prepared to devote time and money to their well being.

PLANT CHOICE

It is probably true to say that choosing plants in small gardens is affected more by climate, aspect, drainage and space than the actual clay soil.

Well managed clay soils will feature a varied and interesting range of plants, far wider than most other soils in fact. For instance, once limed, neutral to acid clays are relatively easy to keep in a suitable state to support lime lovers like clematis and gypsophila. It is less of a risk growing these plants on a neutral to acid clay soil than on a neutral to acid sandy soil which needs constant readjustment. When it comes to lime rich clays, however, the same rules apply as with any other lime rich soil: don't plant acid lovers like rhododendrons and azaleas.

This point needs to be made at the outset: all garden plants come in two categories. First there are the moisture loving marginals and bog plants, and plants like primulas and ferns, which revel in the cool, moist heavy soil. And secondly there are the vast majority of garden-worthy plants, including fruit trees and bushes, which will grow along happily, with a bit of extra help.

Among the ornamentals to avoid for clay soils are those which are recognized as being marginally hardy to the locality concerned. Plants which resent wetness at the roots, especially during the winter months, should also be avoided. Shrubs like sun rose (helianthemum) and broom (cytisus) are two which spring immediately to mind.

As a general rule of thumb guide when choosing food crops, it is best to concentrate on maincrop varieties. The nature of the soil is far from ideal for early crops. But the richness and fertility, with a bit of extra feeding, suit the production of heavier maincrops. Leaf vegetables like brassicas grow very well on clay soils, provided they are generously limed first. Herbs like sage and thyme prefer sandy soils and do less well in clays than the stronger growing mint and parsley. If you want to grow them, pop them in containers or raised beds.

The popular image of planting roses on clay soil as a solution to all problems wants treating with caution. Roses are pest and disease prone, and hard work on any type of soil. However, given plenty of attention and well worked, drained and generously manured beds, roses will undoubtedly grow well on clay.

As indeed will other members of the rose family and related trees and shrubs like mountain ash (rowan), the whitebeams and other sorbus, plum and cherry – and other prunus, flowering quince (chaenomeles), thorns (crataegus), cotoneasters and firethorn (pyracantha). For detailed lists of plants particularly well suited to clay soils see pages 74-103.

SOIL MANAGEMENT TO GET THE BEST OUT OF CLAY

Clay soils have not earned the name 'heavy' without good cause. Under varying weather conditions, wet or dry, they can involve much heavy work. But with a bit of forethought, work planning and careful timing of operations, much can be done to make life easier.

Timing of operations

Initially, until garden clay soils are suitably drained and improved, the opportunities for satisfactorily working the ground are often extremely limited. With wet or freezing conditions in winter, slow drying in spring, and bone hardness in hot summers there would not appear to be a lot of scope for groundwork. As previously indicated, clay soils should never be worked when really wet or dry. In practice, these restrictions on gardening can be greatly reduced by improving the condition of the soil. Clay soils respond favourably, perhaps more so than any other, to good treatment. Draining, manuring, liming as necessary, and generous mulching is time and money well spent, as it will extend the period when groundwork is practical. Take all reasonable steps to improve the texture of heavy clay soils by working in bulky organics at every opportunity, and include some clean coarse sand and fine grit; see pages 112-136.

The age-old practice of digging clay soils in autumn is as sound now as ever it was. Never attempt to dig heavy clay soils in spring or you will risk having lumpy clods of soil all summer long.

Before leaving the important subject of timing, brief reference should be made to the recommended practice of planting trees, shrubs and conifers in spring on heavy soils. Setting out plants in autumn is normally considered best for most soils, but in exposed gardens and where soil can get waterlogged there is much to be said for spring planting using container grown stock. This minimizes the risk of losing plants during winter due to frost heave, exposed roots, or because of suffocation and drowning. Plants which are struggling for survival will almost inevitably die during a hard winter.

Compaction and surface crusting

The formation of a compacted surface crust is a fairly common feature on clay soils, especially where there is high rainfall. This should be prevented whenever possible.

Treading, trampling or barrowing over clay soils at any other time than when they are dry will result in undue compaction and consolidation, resulting in reduced aeration, slow drainage and the likelihood of waterlogging. Keep to the paths whenever possible. And if weeding, pruning, tending plants, manuring or earthmoving makes it necessary to walk over the moist soil, then work from planks. Alternatively put down temporary paths of straw or bark chips. By a similar token, resist the temptation to overfirm the soil when planting on heavy soils as the result is an unacceptable degree of compaction. Bear in mind, clay soils generally provide adequate anchorage for most plants, without the need for firming around the roots.

Water lilies are unsurpassed when it comes to summer colour. Don't allow the foliage to cover more than half the surface area of the pool.

Surface crusting can also be quite a problem on soils around permanent plantings of shrubs and perennials. Clay soils tend to pack down hard and hoeing is not an easy task, forking is not necessarily the answer either. Surface mulching usually provides the key to success – the best type being well rotted farmyard manure or garden compost. When forked in at the end of the season, the surface soil will be found to be friable and more easily worked. Subsequently, where mulching is carried out annually in spring and replenished throughout the growing season, the soil improvement is continued and sustained (see pages 112-16).

Seedbeds need special preparations to overcome the problem of surface crusting. Never, for instance, overfirm the soil. Details of this and other techniques are discussed in pages 52-3. With annual bedding plants and vegetables transplant sturdy container raised plants whenever possible. This is much better than attempting to sow direct.

When it comes to watering, ball watering at the base of plants is more effective than watering over the whole area and creates less risk of compaction. With sprinkler watering, misting is less likely to cause surface crusting than coarse water droplets.

Soil moisture

Many clay soils suffer from an excess of moisture. This provides a vital clue to their successful management. Regulate and control the soil's moisture and the mastery of clay soil comes within your grasp.

Good drainage, as already mentioned, is an important step to improve the soil as is the improvement of the structure. In addition, valuable extra refinements, based on regional customs, have evolved. These practices can make all the difference between success and failure in problem wet sites or in districts of high rainfall, especially where clay soils have not been fully broken in and improved.

In cool, wet districts, where soils are slow to dry out after prolonged rain, growing or planting on raised ridges is worth a try. Waterlogging is avoided as the rainwater drains off the ridges into the furrows alongside. This method when used for growing crops like potatoes, turnips and swedes works well. Planting on ridges is a good idea too when setting out hedging plants in low-lying wet gardens. This can also be

usefully modified and extended to flower beds and tree planting pits. These are raised in the centre, or around the trunk in the case of trees, and allowed to fall away gradually.

A good lawn is an attractive feature in any garden. But on clay soils in wet districts an excellent lawn is never easy to achieve; even a reasonable one can be difficult to establish. Many end up looking more like a quagmire and are of very little use. One way round the problem is to lay new lawns on prepared sand and rubble rafts as this ensures good drainage. Because of the difficulty in obtaining a good seedbed, turfing is always preferable to seeding, when a quick establishment of the grasses becomes possible. Subsequently, a new lawn laid on a free-draining base withstands quite extensive use without showing any signs of excessive wear and tear.

CLAY SOILS AND GARDEN DESIGN

A sound garden design will assist in the achievement of a number of important objectives. It can help to:

(**a**) Make the most of the garden

(**b**) Ensure a practical and attractive layout
(**c**) Minimize maintenance
(**d**) Keep down costs
(**e**) Avoid subsequent problems.

When designing a garden on clay soil it is especially important always to be aware of the nature of the soil itself. Clay soil exerts a powerful influence over many aspects of garden design.

Construction works
All too often clay soils are blamed for all sorts of problems when the fault lies more fairly at the door of bad workmanship, where insufficient attention has been paid to detail. With care and planning, most difficulties with clay soils can be avoided.

Access The matter of access over clay soils is extremely important. They should not be walked over more than necessary and the laying of hard-all-weather paving to all parts of the garden is most strongly advised. Also there is much to be said for hard surfaces which incorporate sitting areas. As the clay expands and contracts on wetting and drying, it is particularly important not to skimp on the foundations when laying hard surfaces. Allow for a generous depth of consolidated hardcore under all paths and drives. A minimum of 10 cm (4 in) is the usual amount for garden paths, ideally overlaid with a 2.5 cm (1 in) minimum concrete mix as a base for the paving slabs. This is a higher specification than is normal on undisturbed gravel soils, or even over undisturbed chalk in low rainfall areas. There are of course many other permutations for path construction – a 6 cm (2½ in) layer of concrete can be laid in situ over the hardcore base.

One detail which is often overlooked is the question of path levels. The usual advice is to set paths about 1 cm (⅜ in) below, say, lawn levels. However, on clay soils it is often better to set the path surface at a similar height *above* the lawn. This helps to reduce surface ponding on paths in wet weather and reduces the likelihood of slime and icy patches in winter. In addition, the use of stepping stones across lawns, and even spacing them strategically in borders, can help to minimize soil puddling.

Walls When constructing walls, or putting up garden buildings, make sure the foundations are laid on firm ground and that you allow adequate depth for them. Always seek professional advice before you start this work. It is false economy not to do so.

With retaining walls, be sure to observe good building guidelines. Make them thick enough and follow the 1:3 rule: this specifies that a wall should be built to a thickness of not less than one third its height. A 90 cm (3 ft) high wall should therefore be not less than 30 cm (12 in) wide at the base (see diagram). Because clay soils are almost invariably wet soils, it is also vital to build retaining walls and terrace supports with an inward tilt. This is to counteract the weight of the wet soil behind the wall. As a useful rule of thumb guide, aim to slope the wall inwards about 2.5-4 cm (1-1½ in) from the vertical for every 30 cm (12 in) in height. Therefore, a 90 cm (3 ft) high wall should be sloped back about 10 cm (4 in) from the vertical (see diagram). Finally, in any terrace or retaining wall provision must be made for adequate drainage or weep holes. This is to relieve any build up of pressure and reduce the weight of soil and water behind the wall (see pages 33).

When constructing earth walls or banks which are unsupported by retaining walls, don't make them steeper than about 1 in 4, as you will risk some landslip.

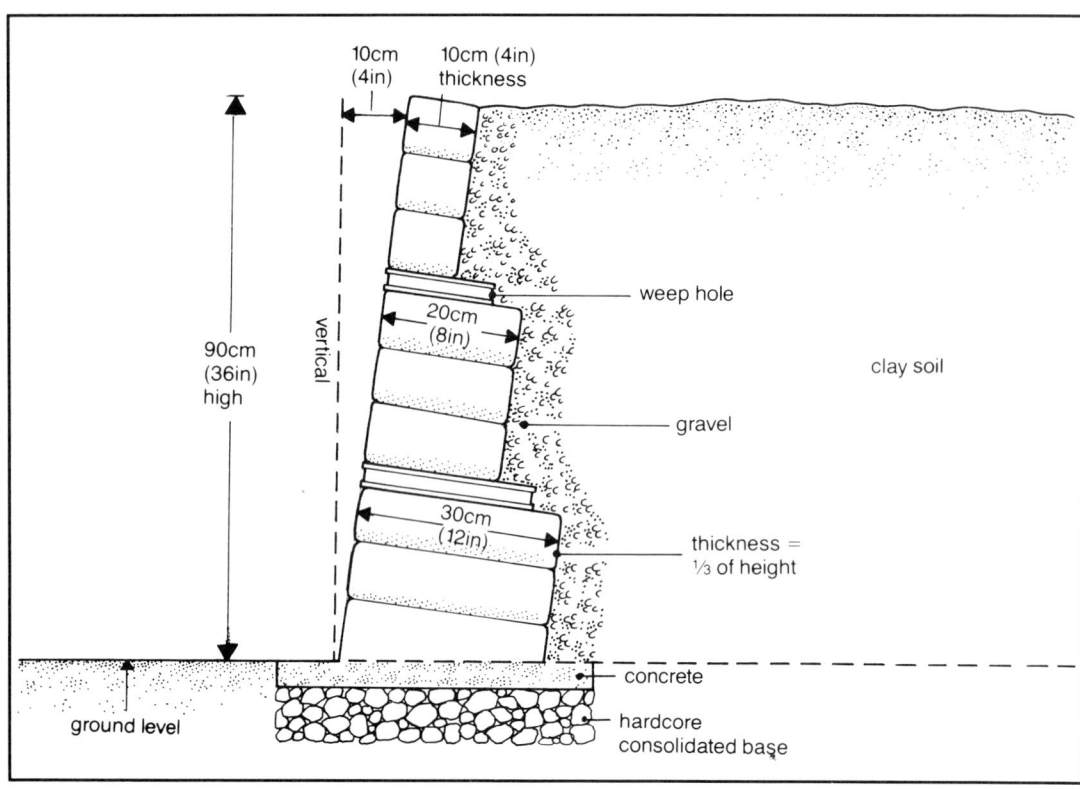

10cm
(4in)

10cm (4in)
thickness

90cm
(36in)
high

vertical

weep hole

20cm
(8in)

clay soil

gravel

30cm
(12in)

thickness =
⅓ of height

concrete

ground level

hardcore
consolidated base

Fig. 2.   Set retaining walls back from the vertical and provide weep holes to allow subsoil water to escape.

Disturbed land When planning a new garden on clay soil after building operations have been completed, do give the ground time to settle first. Where the intention is to lay a new lawn, there is always a strong temptation to roughly level the ground and lay grass as soon as possible, especially if you have children. In this situation, where lawns are made in haste on unsettled, disturbed land, future levelling renovations are going to be needed. Where time and layout allow, the ideal method is to cultivate and level the ground over a two to three month period during summer as this gives time for settlement as well as weedkilling. But it is well appreciated that this is easier said than done. Still on the subject of settlement, it is a mistake to try to put up a glass greenhouse without a purpose-made firm base. If you don't do this you may well end up with needless twisting of the frame and consequent cracking and breaking of glass as the ground expands and contracts. Placed on a substantial base on well constructed foundations, you should have no problems.

Fencing Another common failing arises when putting up garden fences. Where fencing and rustic work looks rather lopsided after high winds, especially in wet weather, the fault is very often due to insufficient depth of the supporting stakes. It can also be caused by a failure at the start to sink the stakes in concrete. Packing stakes firmly with hardcore is adequate to prevent movement on average soils, but not necessarily on clays. When buying stakes allow for about a third to a quarter of the total length to be buried in the ground. Posts for, say, a 1.5 m (5 ft) high fence should be not less than about 2 m, (6½ ft) long. If modern proprietary metal post sockets are used for timber stakes, don't skimp on them. Choose 45 cm (18 in) minimum deep sockets for a 1.5 m (5 ft) fence, or alternatively follow the manufacturer's advice. On clay soils metal sockets really need sinking in concrete to be 100% sure of success.

Drainage This is closely interlinked with garden design and layout because of the slow draining nature of clay soils and the fact that rainwater sinks only slowly into the ground, making the run-off of surface water a problem. In wet districts, and where sudden heavy rains are commonplace, steps need to be taken if flash flooding and erosion of the topsoil are to be avoided.

Surface water run-off is bound up with levels and levelling – in part at least. Where, for example, the garden slopes down to the house surface water will, unless diverted, follow the slope to the lowest point. If this happens to be the house the result is stagnant water and a wet area in the region of the foundations. Problems such as this can be approached from several angles. Terracing can be a solution or contouring the ground across the slope. This slows the downward rush of water allowing more time for it to sink into the ground.

Where terracing or contouring are impractical, for example on neighbouring land, then consider installing interceptor drains. These can simply take the form of French drains, constructed across the slope to trap and divert the water away to a surface outfall (see pages 29-36). Similarly on patios and other large paved areas it is advisable to provide interceptor drains. These again will trap and divert surface water instead of permitting flooding. Another alternative is to make slopes in the ground to alter the direction of water flow to the side of the house or buildings, perhaps. Terracing, contouring and building retaining walls are equally appropriate to small as to large gardens – it is all a question of scale.

Sunken gardens These are not advisable on clay soils because they are likely to end up with too much water and become garden pools. Raised beds are a better bet (see pages 52-3).

Pools and bog gardens The problem of excess water from clay soils can be turned to advantage to make one or more garden pools. But do exercise caution if you decide to do this and build in safeguards in the areas where young children are likely to wander.

In public parks and large gardens it has long been recognized as sound practice to use pools as balancing lakes to prevent uncontrolled flooding. The same idea can be adapted to suit small gardens. In prolonged wet weather, during torrential downpours, and throughout winter, the pool levels rise and accommodate the excess water. On clay soils it is usually a relatively easy matter to create a bog garden alongside – or at one end of the pool. Any surplus water from the pool then finds its way into the bog garden. Pools and bog gardens are regular features of clay soil landscapes. When creating these mini-balancing pools take good care not to divert any polluted, oily water from, say, car washing areas or road water contaminated with salt, as damage will be caused to the plants.

It is perhaps worth mentioning that clay soils can be converted quickly and easily into an impervious pool liner using Bentonite. This is a powder preparation used in the building trade to form lagoons for water storage. In dry weather the pool area is hollowed out with gently sloping sides. A layer of Bentonite is then sprinkled over the whole area and the pool slowly filled. Flexible liners are still more suitable.

Speciality gardens It is a well-established fact that, in the wild, each soil type favours its own characteristic flora—with variations dependent upon sun, shade, shelter and exposure. This theme can be exploited in speciality gardens where the aim is to allow a particular group of plants to dominate the area.

In sunny situations on heavy soils, a rose garden is often suggested. Other possibilities include a paeony collection, a chrysanthemum border, or a perennial border of sun loving plants like heleniums, bergamot, astilbes and asters. A mixed shrub border with dwarf willows, mahonia, red and yellow barked dogwoods, hypericums, viburnums, forsythia, philadelphus and weigela is another popular feature. Around the pool aquatic plants like bog iris thrive.

In sun or partial shade, fruit gardens of currants, gooseberries, raspberries and loganberries can prove successful.

Primulas and ferns are well tried and proven for shady conditions. Collections of mixed shade-tolerant flowering perennials also wear well. Schemes of plants such as ligularia, astilbe and mimulus rarely fail. Groups of foliage plants can make eyecatching displays.

Subsequent management
Sound preparatory work on clay soils is soon undone unless subsequent management is of a sufficiently high standard to maintain the soil's fertility and keep plants healthy. Routine care must be related to the type of soil, plant needs and to the prevailing site conditions (see pages 112-16).

SPECIALITY GARDENS AND PLANT COLLECTIONS FOR CLAY SOILS

Sun	Semi-shade	Shade	Gardens and collections
yes	yes	yes	Astilbe collection
yes	yes	—	Bog garden mixed
yes	yes	—	Bog iris collection
yes	yes	—	Bush and cane fruit garden
yes	yes	—	Chrysanthemum collection
—	yes	yes	Fern collection or garden
yes	yes	—	Flowering shrub collection or border
yes	yes	yes	Foliage garden
yes	yes	—	Hemerocallis collection
—	yes	yes	Hosta collection
yes	yes	—	Paeony collection
yes	yes	—	Perennial border or collection
—	yes	yes	Primula collection or garden
yes	—	—	Rose garden or collection
yes	—	—	Water garden of aquatics and waterlilies

SOIL PREPARATION AND IMPROVEMENT

WHERE TO BEGIN

On moving house it is accepted by most families, especially those with children and pets, that there is a degree of urgency to get the garden in good condition as soon as possible. The starting point will depend on individual circumstances, the prevailing condition of the site and soil, and the time of year. The immediate priorities on an unmade plot and neglected garden will obviously differ from those in a well maintained, existing garden.

But no matter whether the garden is new and unmade, part laid out, neglected, or reasonably well established, a systematic approach to organizing the garden is advisable. Tackling jobs in a logical order, in the right way and at a suitable time can save needless work, frustration, time and expense. There is little to be gained by rushing out on a fine, sunny afternoon and planting some choice tree or shrub in totally unsuitable conditions. By all means, get hold of plants when they

A speciality bed of chrysanthemums is useful for cutting. A careful selection of varieties can provide a succession of bloom. Good drainage is essential.

are obtainable, but if necessary grow them in containers until the ground is *properly* prepared and the conditions are right for planting.

LEVELS AND LEVELLING

When laying out a new garden, one of the first jobs is the provision of paths and drives with new homes, provision is usually the builder's reponsibility. The position of paths and driveways plus roads, patios, buildings, boundaries and existing mature trees, will determine the 'fixed' levels to which the rest of the garden is made (see pages 54-8). It is vital that any necessary levelling is completed early on in the layout and development of a garden on clay. Levels exert an enormous influence on soil drainage, water levels, ground stability and erosion. In consequence, levelling should be attended to before any drainage is attempted.

One thing to decide at the outset of preparing a garden is whether to hire contractors or do the work DIY fashion. One thing you should remember from the start is that dealing with clay soil can be slow, heavy work. Hiring contractors can prove expensive,

but they will certainly get the work done more quickly. However, be sure to discuss exactly what is involved before starting and, more importantly, agree a price. Be wary about employing jobbing labourers, they may seem cheap but will be unskilled in gardening and landscape techniques and have scant knowledge of the problems with clay.

The first thing to do with your site is clear away the rubbish, builder's rubble and unwanted vegetation before contemplating any serious levelling. To minimise the effects of compaction, put down planks to serve as temporary pathways when taking away rubbish and when working the soil.

When levelling clay soils it is imperative to keep the topsoil and subsoil separate; never bury valuable topsoil under stiff clay subsoil.

Major levelling With changes in level of 8 cm (3 in) and more, it is a good idea to level the area in strips of convenient width – 90 cm (3 ft) wide is about right. This makes it easier to work and keeps earth moving to a minimum. Remove and stack the topsoil, then set about levelling the subsoil working to pegs hammered in at predetermined levels. Use the cut-and-fill method wherever possible, this also helps to cut down on earth moving. In essence, low spots are raised with surplus soil dug out from the higher areas. Once the subsoil is completely level, cover over evenly with topsoil from the second strip. The process is repeated until eventually, the topsoil from the first strip is used to infill the last. When raising the levels, remember to make allowances for settlement. It is likely to be in the region of 20% over a two year period. If you are not experienced, leave major levelling work to the professionals who know how to work quickly and efficiently.

Minor levelling For changes in level of less than 8 cm (3 in), it is quicker, easier and quite satisfactory just to surface cut-and-fill. If the soil cut away from the high spots is insufficient to raise the levels, you can just import more topsoil.

Levelling near buildings Never pile soil above the damp-proof course, always aim to keep it 15 cm (6 in) above the soil.

Levelling lawns Aim for a minimum slope of 1 in 80 to prevent any waterlogging and achieve a maximum slope of 1 in 4 for ease of management and mowing. Gradients steeper than 1 in 4 are better terraced to avoid the risk of excessive rainwater run-off and consequent erosion.

Terracing is difficult work to do and is best left to qualified, reputable contractors. Don't consider carrying out the work yourself without professional on-the-spot advice.

Contouring Where planted areas are envisaged on relatively steep sloping ground, plan them across the line of fall. The same goes for terracing and helps to stabilize erosion from higher ground. Grass and spreading dwarf groundcover like periwinkle (vinca) and *Cotoneaster dammeri,* bind the soil and help considerably in the slowing down of erosion.

SOIL DRAINAGE

For many plants set out on clay soils, adequate drainage makes all the difference between gardening success and failure. But there are also other points to bear in mind: well-drained soils are more manageable and can be cultivated more easily with much less reliance on good weather.

An effective drainage system is most likely to be achieved by a combination of construction works and cultivation methods. In fact, soil drainage is usually best tackled from three angles:

1 Provide subsoil/underground drainage. But to install any effective subsoil drainage system several conditions need to be satisfied: the surface water should be able to reach the subsoil drain reasonably quickly. This will only happen if the soil structure and condition are good enough to allow percolation (see point 2); the drains should be suitably positioned, not too deep and not too distant (see below); the drainage system should be adequate to cope with the volume of incoming water and should have a suitable outlet.

2 The surface to subsoil drainage achieved via soil improvement. All too frequently, soil improvement doesn't receive the attention it deserves.

3 This last, and largely neglected, angle for dealing with drainage is to intercept and divert incoming water. Run-off water from hard surfaced areas like driveways and patios; spasmodic deluges from roofs devoid of gutters and downspouts; and drainage water from neighbouring land, can all add unnecessarily to the problems of slow draining clay soils.

Subsoil drainage systems

The choice of drainage system and its final design should be related to individual circumstances and to the availability and cost of materials.

Assuming it has been established that the soil is clay or heavy loam, it is not usual to test for water levels. But if you are not sure, dig a test hole in a low spot in the garden. Excavate the hole to about 35 cm (14 in) square and 45 cm (14 in) deep. Cover the hole with a sheet of rigid plastic, or a dustbin lid, and examine the hole at regular intervals throughout winter, especially after heavy rain. Replace the cover promptly each time to exclude the rainwater. If water does collect in the hole and rises to within 20-25 cm (8-10 in) of the surface, drainage is essential for most garden plants to survive.

Tile drainage This traditional farming system consists of a herringbone arrangement of 8-10 cm (3-4 in) porous earthenware drain pipes. These are laid out on a bed of gravel, no more than 60 cm (2 ft) deep and no more than 3 m (10 ft) apart, but this system needs modifying to suit a small suburban garden. On farms the pipes are usually laid with a fall of 1 in 80 to drain into an open ditch or water course. In the average garden there are neither ditches nor water courses, and obstacles like buildings, paths and walls have to be contended with. One useful compromise is to combine a modified tile drainage system with a rubble-filled sump drain (see below).

Continuous pipe system
The introduction of perforated plastic drainpipes has revolutionized, speeded up and cut the cost of agricultural land drainage. This is also having a rub-off effect on small scale drainage schemes in private gardens where plastic piping is now being increasingly used. Round 5 cm (2 in) piping is the most commonly used and it looks rather like a giant hose pipe. Variations of this type are coming onto the market all the time. All are bedded in gravel and set at a similar depth and falls as for tile drains. They should however be set closer together because they are a smaller bore – at no more than 2-2.5 m (7-8 ft) apart.

Rubble-filled sump In small gardens, rubble-filled sumps are usually a most practical and successful method of sub-soil drainage. They are quite simple and easy to construct and involve making holes of 90 cm (3 ft) square and of similar depth at obvious low points and trouble spots in the garden. This work really needs to be done in fine weather, and the topsoil needs to be kept to one side. The holes should then be part-filled with clean builder's rubble to within 30 cm (12 in) of the surface and be firmed and consolidated as the filling proceeds. The rubble then needs to be covered with a 2.5-4 cm (1-1½ in) layer of fine gravel (to help prevent wash down of soil) before topping off with good topsoil. One sump will normally drain an area of about 14-22 sq m (16-25 sq yds) of clay soil.

Sump and pipe systems
These are extensions of the rubble-filled sumps. Drainage tiles or plastic pipes are laid to discharge drainage water into the sump. The tiles or pipes are bedded in gravel and provide an increased surface area for water collection. This is a most efficient drainage system, which is particularly suited to stiff clays. Set the tiles or pipes no more than about 45 cm (18 in) deep where they enter the sump;

Fig. 3.   Drain pipes discharging water into rubble sumps drain heavy soils efficiently.

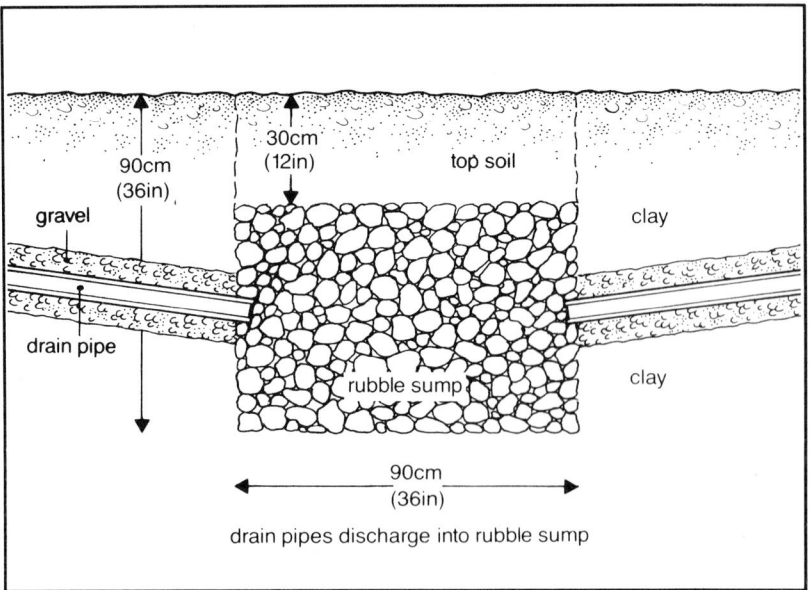

drain pipes discharge into rubble sump

and allow them to rise about 5 cm (2 in) in 3 m (10 ft) to the extremities of the area being drained.

Gravel raft This works on the same principle as a rubble-filled sump except gravel is used instead of rubble. It is a system that is of particular significance in areas of high rainfall.

Lawns which are laid on stiff clay are liable to become a mass of muddy footprints; they fail to stand up to wear in wet, or even showery weather. This is obviously a serious defect in any garden, but even more disastrous in a small garden where young children have limited play space. Fortunately, the prob-lem can be resolved, to a large extent, by laying the lawn on a gravel raft. The topsoil is carefully removed from the lawn area and stacked to one side. The subsoil base needs to be levelled out with all humps and hollows removed and all-owing a minimum fall of 1 in 80 away from the house to shed surface water. A 13 cm (5 in) layer of gravel is then spread out over the base and firmed up. This is followed with a 3 cm (1 in) layer of sand, and topped with about 10 cm (4 in) of prepared top-soil (see Fig. 4). The depth of topsoil is adjusted to bring the lawn level to within 5 cm (2 in) of the surrounding paths, ready for turfing. This makes allowances for standard turves of 4 cm (1½ in) thickness.

Gravel rafts may sound like a lot of work and expense, but in a small garden it is not as forbidding as it sounds. The subsequent extra wear and tear that the lawn can then take is well worth the time and effort. Incidently, many bowling greens are constructed on roughly similar lines enabling them to withstand play in damp weather. Raised beds are also often made up on a gravel base.

Weepholes and gravel
Wherever terracing is employed it is important to provide weep holes in the retaining walls to allow the subsoil water to escape. As an approximate guide, allow a 5 cm (2 in) weep-pipe per m (3¼ ft) run of 60 cm (2 ft) high vertical wall. Failure to install weepholes can result in complete collapse of the retaining wall. To ensure improved drainage always line the back of retaining walls with a 10 cm (4 in) thick layer of clean rubble. This is vital where retaining walls are 90 cm (3 ft) or more in height.

Surface to subsoil drainage
Heavy clay soils are notorious for the slow movement of water from the surface, through the topsoil, and down to the subsoil drains. It is not uncommon for these soils to be waterlogged at or near the surface, and the subsoil drains to be clear of standing water. This is largely due to

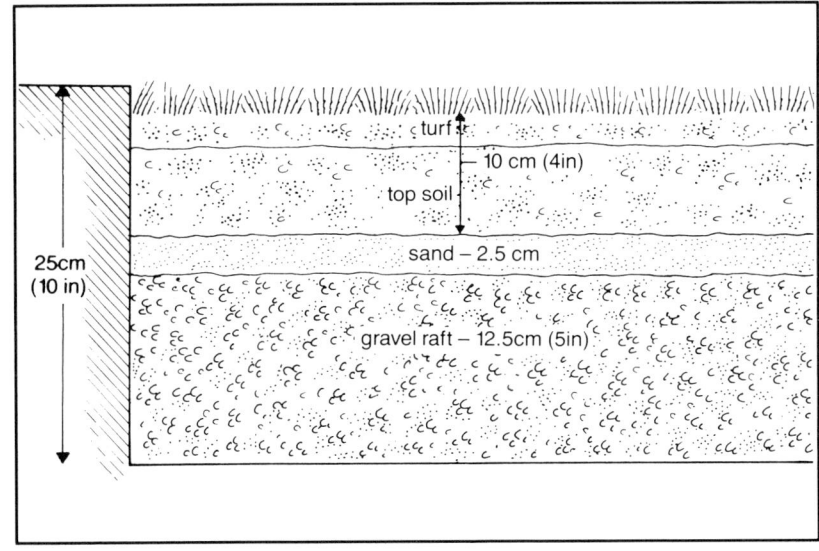

Fig. 4.   Lay lawns on rubble rafts and they will stand up better to wear and tear.

surface crusting and compaction of the soil. Given time, the problem can usually be overcome by routine soil cultivation together with generous manuring and liming. However, in exceptional circumstances, it is sometimes necessary to make special provision to speed up the downward movement of water. This is definitely needed when incoming surface water from neighbouring land is causing a nuisance.

Rubble trench One of the quickest and most effective ways of getting surface water down to the subsoil drains is by means of open or French drains. More sophisticated forms of these can often be seen on motorway embankments when you are driving along. In the garden situation they are constructed by digging out trenches, about 30 cm (12 in) wide and 45-60 cm (1½-2 ft) deep. The trenches are then filled to within 2.5 cm (1 in) or so of the surface with clean rubble and topped up with fine gravel; this helps to permit uninterrupted water percolation.

Rubble trenches are useful in any part of the garden where water is likely to collect such as: alongside patios and driveways; at the base of slopes; at the base of retain-

ing walls; in low spots.

Brushwood is sometimes advocated as an alternative to rubble and gravel. But a word of caution: it is not very good to use as it not only rots in time, but it can also harbour pests and diseases.

Straw walling This is an almost forgotten practice, but it still has a place – particularly in new gardens where soil conditions have yet to be improved.

With crops like runner beans, tomatoes and sweet peas, which need generous watering in dry weather, surface ponding can be very restricting. This is where clean straw, uncontaminated with weedkillers, can be of some help. Using a spade, make a 30 cm (12 in) deep 'V'-shaped trench alongside each row of plants. Force wedges of straw into the trench with the aid of the spade as this aids the downward movement of water. As the straw decomposes, some nitrogen is robbed from the soil due to bacterial action. Anticipate this action and apply a bit of extra balanced fertilizer before planting crops like tomatoes.

Interceptor drains and water diversion In gardens all too often little attention is given to diverting and chan-

When massed, day lilies (hemerocallis) are outstanding. These showy and spectacular clump formers are grown for their lily-like flowers produced in long succession during summer.

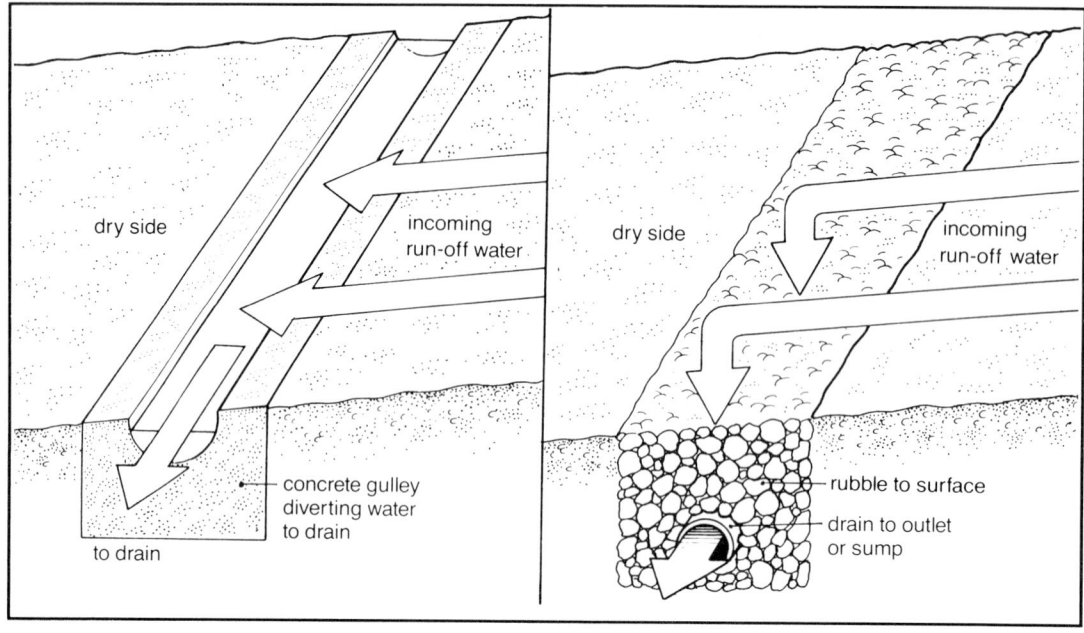

Fig. 5. Anticipate nuisance by channelling away excess surface water in rubble drains and concrete gulleys.

nelling away excess water as a preventive measure. Because of this many gardening opportunities are lost.

Concrete gulleys or channels, built into patios and driveways, which discharge water down service drains can help to solve the problem. Open rubble ditches alongside neighbouring land with suitable outlets is also sometimes a possibility. Well sited rubble drains with porous tiles or plastic pipes embedded in the bottom can also work well. All sheds, buildings, greenhouses and other outbuildings should be fitted with leakproof guttering and downspouts leading to existing drains or rainwater collecting butts.

CHOOSING AND USING BULKY ORGANICS

When it comes to the general improvement of clay soils, a heavy reliance is put on substantial applications of bulky organics like manures, garden compost and peat.

Obtaining enough bulky organics at a reasonable cost often proves to be the limiting factor in soil improvement. But assuming supplies are available and heavy applications are made, the fertility of clay soil is enhanced in several ways: aeration is improved; surface water percolates more quickly down to subsoil drains (see page 30); soil stickiness is also reduced and the crumb structure is improved for easier cultivation; soils are darkened, and combined with improved percolation warm up more quickly in spring; manures and composts supply valuable plant nutrients.

The choice
Garden compost is often readily available and one of the best bulky organics around. The main problem is making enough to suit the garden needs. Be prepared to buy some clean straw and bracken to help make up the bulk. When well made, garden compost is at least as rich in nutrients as farmyard manure.

Manure At one time, farmyard manure formed the backbone of bulky organics in most gardens. Now, because of expense, availability and transport problems it is bought mainly by gardeners to eke out the supplies of garden compost. Strawy horse manure is the first choice for clay soils, but cow and pig manure make valuable alternatives. As mentioned previously farmyard manure does contain valuable nutrients. Poultry manures even tend to be too rich to apply in quantity as bulky soil conditioners – they are best reserved for use as fertilizers.

When buying manure be wary of purchasing any which might have been contaminated with antibiotics or other animal medication. Also try to avoid manures where weedkillers or chemically-treated straw were used for bedding down the animals. The ones containing raw sawdust and wood shavings are also best given a miss because of the risk of importing disease and attracting ants and woodlice.

Leafmould Where supplies of well rotted, composted leaves are obtainable at low cost they are a worthwhile proposition. If you have an abundance of leaves in your garden compost them, but first check that street sweepings from busy roads have not been included. These will often have high levels of other pollutants and are unsuitable for food production.

Mushroom compost is a local product, often available in plentiful supplies at a reasonable cost. It is mainly composed of composted straw or manure with added chalk and peat. Used raw, it is best reserved for acid or neutral soils because of the likely high lime content. Mix the compost thoroughly with other vegetable waste before applying to chalky soils.

Peat Granulated, fibrous sphagnum and sedge peats are useful for improving clay soils, but they don't come cheap. Very fine dusty, or greasy sedge peats are not suitable for clay soils. Sphagnum peats are inclined to be acid, so there might be a need for liming if used on acid clays. Sphagnum peat is an important constituent of potting compost prepared for containers and raised beds. Peats provide minimal nutrients, but they do burn up slowly, giving lasting benefit to the soil.

Barks Proprietary composted and pulverised barks make good soil conditioners and because of this are getting more popular and more expensive. They are slow to rot down and they have certain similarities to peat. Pulverised barks tend to cause temporary nitrogen deficiency after spreading, and you will need to add some extra fertilizer to compensate for this.

Other organics Explore the local availability of products like spent hops, bracken, straw, seaweed, municipal compost and sewage sludge, which will all add bulk to the compost heap. Buy sewage sludge that is not contaminated with heavy metals like zinc and cadmium, which prove toxic to both plant and animal life. Also beware of any broken glass in the municipal compost, and check that the straw has not been treated with any chemicals.

How to use them
Make the most of bulky organics by spreading them sensibly and in conjunction with other soil conditioners and fertilizers. Generally speaking, bulky organics are either dug or forked into the ground directly as soil conditioners. They can also be applied as a surface mulch (see pages 112-16).

How to apply as soil conditioners The ideal way of incorporating bulky organics into the soil must be geared to their type and condition. Basically, they should be applied to the soil in autumn when digging beds and borders, and at planting time in the autumn or spring.

When digging aim to spread well-rotted compost or manure into the bottom of each trench after loosening up the soil and do the same with planting holes. Planting pockets for trees and shrubs in the spring should be treated in the same way with well rotted materials. However, as a second best alternative on

Single paeonies flower freely, but the charm of the double cottage garden varieties are hard to beat on clay soil. They need sunny, sheltered positions.

clay soils it is quite acceptable to apply long, strawy part-decomposed manure or compost in the autumn. Make sure it is well buried and a general fertilizer like Growmore is scattered all over, at the rate of a small handful per sq m (1 sq yd) to hasten breakdown and to prevent any nitrogen depletion. It is better to do this than wait until materials are well decomposed, and possibly delay any treatment by a year.

When preparing for shallow rooting of bedding plants and salad crops in the spring, peat, leafmould or composted bark can be lightly forked, or raked into the top 5-10 cm (2-4 in) of soil.

Rates of application These will obviously vary depending on supplies and the condition of the soil. When breaking in new ground—which is going to take up to five years—aim to use the equivalent of an 8 cm (3 in) layer of compost, manure or leafmould spread over the entire area. With peat and composted or pulverized bark a 5 cm (2 in) layer will suffice. Thereafter an annual dressing of any of these bulky organics at the rate of one to two buckets [9 litre (2 gallon) bucket] per sq m (1 sq yd) should be adequate.

COMPOSTING

All too often the physical condition and nutrient quality of compost is not as good as it should be. Well-made compost, ready for use, should be dark brown, friable and crumbly with a sweet earthy smell.

Although on clay soils it is the physical considerations which are of overiding importance with compost, the nutrient value should not be ignored. After all, 1 tonne (1 ton) of properly made compost contains the equivalent of about 45 kg (100 lb) of general fertilizer. It is also worth remembering that unprotected, uncovered compost can lose 50% of its nutrients due to leaching by rainfall.

To make good compost it is vital to create the right degree of warmth, moisture and aeration so that micro-organisms will thrive and break down the vegetable waste. Although with experience, excellent compost can be made in free-standing heaps, they can often be very untidy. Purpose made compost bins are neat to look at and reduce problems.

In order to make sufficient compost to break in clay soil and maintain fertility, be prepared to set aside a substantial area for storing compost bins – a minimum of two largish bins is called for. This allows for one bin to be filled while the other is left to mature. Bins of 1 cu m (1 cu yd) capacity are the ideal size, and often these are only available in timber. Standard plastic bins are available but are usually much smaller, so more will be needed. These bins are also slower to heat up, so the compost will take longer to make. Choose bins with no bottoms, not only can they be lifted off for ease of emptying, but when placed on a free-drainage gravel base you avoid stagnation in the bottom.

Using a shredder to chop up coarse materials will hasten the composting process. They are expensive to buy, but this is justified when dealing with the vast quantities of compost needed for the improvement of clay soil.

Compost materials

To make good fibrous, trouble-free compost, it pays to be particular about selecting suitable materials. From the start you should avoid using anything which is disease or pest infested; persistent weeds like dock, nettle, bellbine and ground elder; hard, woody stemmed remains; and chemically treated grass clippings or other vegetation. Always try to include healthy vegetable waste including weed and flower remains; grass clippings; household vegetable trimmings; chopped pea and bean haulms, and bulky materials like straw, seaweed, spent hops and mushroom compost.

Although most vegetable waste will rot down in time, weed seeds are always a gamble, so avoid using mature weeds which are seeding. Try not to add too many of one type of material at any time. If you add too much grass clippings, for instance, they will settle down to form a poultice-like mass.

Making garden compost

Most compost heaps and bins are made up on the sandwich principle. Basically, 10-15 cm (4-6 in) layers of mixed vegetable waste are alternated with activator. If the mixture is very dry, water each layer of waste before applying proprietary activator following the manufacturer's recommendation. Poultry droppings or other manure can be used as an alternative to proprietary activator. If you use this method, it is important to replace some of the manure applications with a scattering of ground limestone as filling proceeds. Layer up the compost heap as garden waste becomes available until the heap or bin is complete, keeping it covered in between trips. Finally, cover over and leave to rot down completely. Compost layered during the spring should be ready for use by autumn. Autumn made compost takes longer, as rotting down is slower during the low winter temperatures, but it should be ready for summer mulching.

Leafmould

Don't waste any available deciduous leaves. They are slow to rot down, however, and are best composted separately into leafmould. They will take about two years to decompose sufficiently for use. Evergreen leaves like those of laurel and conifers are not suitable for inclusion in compost.

Make leafmould in a pen made from chicken wire attached to posts. This is adequate to keep the leaves tidy and prevent them blowing about. A useful size is about 1.2 m (4 ft) square by 90 cm (3 ft) high. To hasten the decomposition, sprinkle on a handful of general fertilizer after every 15 cm (6 in) layer of leaves and add a scattering of soil. Finally cover over the whole area with a 3 cm (1 in) layer of fine soil, heaped in a slightly domed shape. Protect the leafmould with a weighted down sheet of plastic and examine occasionally, watering if too dry.

GREEN MANURING

The practice of growing a quick crop and then digging it into the soil to improve fertility has very definite benefits on clay soils. Admittedly, it is not terribly practical in small areas and not a great deal of organic matter is provided, but it is a practice worthy of consideration nonetheless. One of the chief benefits comes from the roots as they force their way through the soil to break it up and improve crumb structure.

Useful green crops to try

The versatile astilbes are noted for their conspicuous, distinctive, brightly coloured mid- to late summer blooms, usually complemented by pleasing foliage before, during and after flowering.

Green manuring mixture	Sow 50g per sq m (1¾ oz per sq yd)
Mustard	Sow 35g per 5 sq m (1 oz per 5 sq yd)
Red clover	Sow 35g per 10 sq m (1 oz per 10 sq yd)
Ryegrass	Sow 35g per sq m (1 oz per sq yd)
Winter vetch/tares	Sow 35g per 3 sq m (1 oz per 3 sq yd)

are: mustard, red clover, ryegrass, green manure mix and winter vetch or tares. Sow in the late spring or summer and then dig in before flowering begins or the stems become too hard and tough. Immediately before digging in, apply 70 g per sq m (2 oz per sq yd) of general fertilizer to prevent any nitrogen depletion.

OTHER SOIL CONDITIONERS

In addition to the bulky organics already discussed, other materials also have a part to play in the improvement of the texture of clay soils. Some have an opening or lightening effect and the way in which this is achieved depends very much on the material itself. Sand and gravel work by diluting the extremely fine grains of clay with their larger, coarser grains of sand and stone. In effect, this mixing brings about a physical change in the soil composition. This is a lasting change which is capable of being further improved by regular annual applications. Other materials can bring about changes chemically. Gypsum (calcium sulphate) and other calcium compounds including lime, act directly on the fine clay particles making them flocculate – form crumb-like aggregates. Each crumb is composed of numerous fine particles which are securely

---

WIDELY USED SOIL CONDITIONERS (LIME EXCLUDED)

Type	Comment
Grit physical	For best results use acid/neutral grits and bear in mind limestone grits are alkaline. Rate as for sand.
Gypsum chemical	A calcium compound verging on neutral. It forms water-stable crumbs. Apply 300 g per sq m (8 oz per sq yd)
Perlite physical	Derived from volcanic rock, it is lightweight, granular and sterile. Near neutral. Used mainly in potting composts, but suitable for seedbed preparation at 9 l (2 gal) per sq m (sq yd).

Sand physical	Coarse grit, river and washed quarry sands are ideal. Avoid fine sand and sea washed sand which contains sodium and will cause stickiness. Apply 1-2 buckets per sq m (sq yd).
Vermiculite physical	The same as perlite, but darker in colour and ultra lightweight. Some samples are alkaline.
Terra Green (Arcillite – a fine, grit-like material) physical	A sterile granular mineral, which is absorbent and moderately acid. Use in the same way as perlite.

held together. Most of the proprietary clay soil improvers you buy in the shops work on this principle. These chemical changes are relatively short lasting and will only suffice for two seasons at the most.

Both physical and chemical conditioners are normally applied either when manuring or when preparing the ground for sowing and planting. They are lightly forked or raked into the top 8-10 cm (3-4 in) of topsoil.

LIME – pH AND LIMING

The status of clay soils varies from acid/lime deficient to alkaline/lime or sodium rich. The degree of activity is expressed on the pH scale by gardeners and scientists alike. A pH reading of 7 is neutral, below is acid and a higher reading is alkaline.

The importance of acidity or alkalinity when gardening on clay is that acid soils below about pH 5.5 and alkaline ones above 7.5, are infertile to the majority of plants. This is because firstly many clay soils are inclined to be extra sticky when highly alkaline, especially if this is due to high soil levels of sodium. Secondly, soil nutrients like nitrogen, phosphorus and potassium, and trace elements like iron and magnesium, become 'fixed' and are not released to plants under very acid or very alkaline conditions.

It must be emphasized that plants vary in their ability to grow in soils of differing pH status. Lime haters like rhododendrons begin to suffer with a pH above 6.5. Lime lovers like clematis suffer with a pH below 6.5.

SOIL TESTING FOR PH

It is not normally necessary to go to the expense of seeking a laboratory analysis for soil. The use of an inexpensive chemical DIY soil test kit is more than adequate. Full instructions are given on how to use the kit and the results are read off on a colour comparison chart. You then follow the recommended application rates which vary according to soil type and crops grown. The accuracy of the test depends to a large extent on how the soil samples are taken. A series of samples should be sought from different parts of the garden, at a depth of 15 cm (6 in), they must all be mixed together thoroughly before testing.

Another popular means of soil testing is with a direct dial soil test meter. A metal probe is pushed into the moist soil and the pH level is read off on a calibrated dial. Unfortunately, the cheaper end of this range can give less accurate readings than the chemical kits discussed above.

Lime application

Ground limestone is the main form of lime sold to correct soil acidity and consists mainly of calcium carbonate. Dolomite limestone, which contains both magnesium and calcium carbonate, is another good alternative. It is recommended for use where magnesium deficiency is a problem. Hydrated lime, a third option, contains calcium hydroxide and has a higher neutralising effect than the other forms, but unfortunately is caustic and unpleasant to handle.

The lime requirement of a soil is usually expressed as the amount of lime needed to raise the soil pH to 6.5. The

Gunnera manicata has handsome, giant rhubarb-like leaves with rich olive green flowers carried on spikes. A plant for large gardens and moist soil.

APPROXIMATE LIME APPLICATIONS
To raise pH of clay soils to 6.5 – g per sq m (oz per sq yd)

Lime type	Existing pH	
	6	5.5
Dolomite limestone	280 (8)	560 (16)
Ground limestone	280 (8)	560 (16)
Hydrated lime	210 (6)	420 (12)

lower the pH the greater the amount of lime is needed.

WHEN AND WHAT TO APPLY?

In the vegetable garden it is normal to apply lime one year in three on a rotational basis. In practice this usually means liming the third of the plot each year which is to grow brassicas.

In the flower garden, and with permanent plantings of perennial shrubs and fruit trees, aim to raise the pH to the optimum level and then top it up annually with small amounts of lime. An average dressing would be 70 g per sq m (2 oz per sq yd). Of course when growing lime haters like rhododendrons, camellias and heathers, liming is omitted. Light applications of gypsum will, however, improve and maintain soil condition in this situation.

In fact where stickiness is a major problem, always combine liming with applications of gypsum. For instance, dressings of dolomite limestone and gypsum on a 1:3 ratio by weight will work wonders. Apply the mixture annually, at the rate of 280-420 g per sq m (8-12 oz per sq yd), for two or three years. Gypsum is also safer to use than carbonate forms of lime in areas of the country with high salinity.

Lime on its own, and when combined with gypsum, is applied in the autumn, with the spring as second best. Scatter dressings thinly over the soil after digging or ridging and leave for the rain to wash in during the winter months. Spring applications are hoed or raked in as soil conditions allow.

Avoid applying lime at the same time as manures or fertilizers: always allow an interval of two or three weeks before you apply.

PREPLANTING CULTIVATIONS

The traditional and best way of breaking in uncultivated clay soil is digging in some form or other. When digging aim to expose as great a surface area of soil as possible to the weathering of frost, wind, rain and sun. This should be left for as long a period as possible; if possible try and complete all digging before winter sets in. By doing this, clods of earth will almost certainly break down into workable soil by the spring. The harder the frosts the easier the job is then likely to be.

Double digging Deep digging is strongly advocated on clay soils, especially in the initial stages. Ignore the modern trend towards shallow cultivations. Deep digging helps to break up chemicals, and physical hard pans (see page 13), improves the surface for subsoil drainage and encourages deeper rooting which increases drought resistance.

There is no getting away from it, digging on clay soil is hard work. Be resigned to digging in short spells; never attempt a long session, especially if new to the scene, as you will soon exhaust yourself. From long experience of working such soils there are no satisfactory shortcuts, but there are ways to ease and speed up the workload. Ideally buy a good, although these can be expensive, stainless steel spade, as the clay is least likely to stick to this type. Forget any ideas of going for pivotted-spades or other gimmicks which claim to avoid lifting – you'll find that they just won't work well on clay.

Specialist clay spades with pointed digging edges are worth seeking out. If you're unaccustomed to digging buy a smaller 'border' spade. Also well worth consideration as an alternative to a spade, is a broad-pronged digging fork. These are lighter to use than a spade and clay sticking is less of a problem. Never attempt to dig the ground with a rusty spade, sand it down first, and keep it well oiled when not in use.

When double digging, the often quoted advice of taking out a trench is best ignored, unless you're looking for extra work. Easier by far is to dig the ground in 60 cm (2 ft) squares. Start by skimming off the weeds, then excavate a hole 60 cm (2 ft) square by 25 cm (10 in) deep, and set the soil to one side, keeping the topsoil separate. Then fork up the subsoil to a depth of about 25 cm (10 in) before spreading a generous layer of manure or garden compost evenly all over the surface.

Next dig out a second 60 cm (2 ft) square, throwing the soil forward to cover the manure or compost in the first hole. Carefully invert each spade or forkful and keep the soil surface reasonably level, making sure you don't break down the lumps too finely. It is far preferable to allow the sun, wind, rain and frost to do this for you. Continue to repeat the process across the patch, forking up the base of the second square, manuring, then filling with inverted soil from the third and so on until the last square has been taken out. This is then filled with soil from the first hole that was dug.

Normal digging is used primarily on the vegetable plot where it can replace double digging two years out of three, once the soil is broken in. Carry out in the same way as double digging but don't fork up the subsoil.

Ridging goes hand in glove with clay soil management. It is the ideal way to expose the maximum surface area of soil to weathering. Ridge the ground in strips, starting as for double digging by taking out a 25 cm (10 in) deep, 60 cm (2 ft) square. Again fork up the bottom and cover generously with some maure or compost. It is important that the soil from the second square is dug out in three spade or fork width strips. Soil from the first strip is inverted a spade or forkful at a time, centrally along the bottom of the first square. Soil from the other two strips goes to the left and to the right, inverted, tilted to tip and slope away from the centre, forming a wide ridge (see diagram opposite). The process is repeated in 60 cm (2 ft) squares, until the whole area is ridged.

Trenching This is worth considering for runner beans, sweet peas, chrysanthemums, dahlias and hedging. It is less work than double digging or ridging the whole area and you will find that it also makes for more economical use of the manure.

Trenching, like digging, is best completed in the autumn. Mark and dig out a trench some 40-60 cm (16-24 in) wide and a spade or fork depth. Set the topsoil to one side and then spread manure or compost in the bottom of the trench and fork it in well. Add more manure and cover over with topsoil to half fill the trench. Leave during the winter months to weather, and in the spring, as soon as the ground is dry enough, fill up the trench with the remaining topsoil and prepare for planting.

> **NOTE**
> When double digging, normal digging and ridging stiff clay, if the layer of topsoil is less than 30 cm (8 in), reduce the excavating depth. Don't attempt to bring up more than about 5 cm (2 in) of clay subsoil to mix in with the topsoil in any one year. It is much better to gradually increase the depth of fertile topsoil over a number of years.
>
> Where the bed system of growing is adopted in, say, the vegetable garden, economize on manure and labour by not digging or manuring the paths.

The moisture garden at Wisley is worth a visit. Seen here near the water's edge are plantings of bog iris, primulas and contrasting foliage plants.

PREPLANTING OPERATIONS

Clay burning

Although rarely carried out these days, clay burning can still be of benefit on heavy soils. But there are two essential requirements: first there must be a large quantity of brushwood to dispose of; secondly, bonfires must be permissable. Burn the brushwood until there is a big bed of red hot ashes. Make up the fire further with more brushwood and cover promptly with a 5 cm (2 in) layer of clay subsoil, leaving air holes at top and bottom (see diagram). When the fire has burnt out, and the clay has cooled, scatter it over some ground waiting to be dug. It has a remarkable lightening effect.

Seedbed preparations

Clay soils are notoriously difficult to work down to a crumbly tilth, suitable for seed sowing, without a lot of hard work and effort. Two golden rules to observe are: work from planks or paths at all times; and avoid overfirming the soil at all costs.

Transplanted crops like brassicas, leeks, lettuce, wallflowers, forget-me-nots and pansies should be sown in containers of seed compost for the first few years at least, and it can be continued longer. Plants are pricked out into larger containers or into raised beds and grown on prior to setting out. Some people prefer the method of sowing direct into raised beds, which also proves successful.

Preparing a raised seedbed Start with 15 cm (6 in) deep timber sides (see diagram). A bed of about 1.2 m (4 ft) square is a good size to start with. Dig out 8 cm (3 in) of soil and replace with 5 cm (2 in) of fine gravel topped off with a 2.5 cm (1 in) layer of coarse sand. Next make up a seedbed mix of two parts good topsoil (imported if need be), plus one part each of granulated sphagnum peat and coarse sand. Work the parts out by volume. Spread the mix out in the raised bed, to a depth of 10-15 cm (4-6 in) and almost level with the board tops. Rake in 70 g per sq m (2 oz per sq yd) of ground limestone. Allow the bed to settle for 14 to 21 days. Then rake in 70 g per sq m (2 oz per sq yd) of general fertilizer like John Innes base or Growmore. Once prepared, a raised bed should last up to six years, provided the losses of topsoil and fertilizer are made good, and the timbers treated with preservative.

Thinned crops When sowing crops in situ to thin, beet and spinach for example, rake the soil level and take out a shallow 'V' shaped furrow of about 1-2 cm (½-¾ in) in depth and line with moist seed compost. Sow the seeds normally and cover with more seed compost. Crops like turnips and swedes are treated in a similar way but are sown on 15-20 cm (6-8 in) high ridges.

Salad crops of lettuce, spring onions, radish and similar vegetables all do well grown to maturity in raised seed beds.

Potatoes are not an ideal crop to grow on clay soils. But if they are grown set them in shallow furrows and earth up around them to keep the tubers drier and warmer.

Final preparations for planting in beds in spring

Working from paths alongside the planting area, or from planks where the beds are too wide, the first job is to carefully level all the ridges and to break up hard clods of earth with the back of a fork. Cultivate lightly and spread preplanting base dressings of general fertilizer at the rate of 110-140 g per sq m (3-4 oz per sq yd), and rake down the soil. If it is inclined to be very sticky, rake in some extra sand. In wet districts it is common practice to earth up beds into a shallow dome, to shed water (see page 51).

Final preparations for turfing

A firm level base must be ensured before you start. Firming the soil by alternating treading heel and toe fashion with raking is best completed in late summer in readiness for autumn turfing. Rake in preturfing fertilizer at the rate of 70 g per sq m (2½ oz per sq yd) (see also page 108).

Planting pockets for trees, shrubs and rock plants are prepared at planting time (see pages 66-73).

Fig. 6. A raised seedbed is useful for seed sowing and for pricking out transplanted vegetable crops and bedding plants.

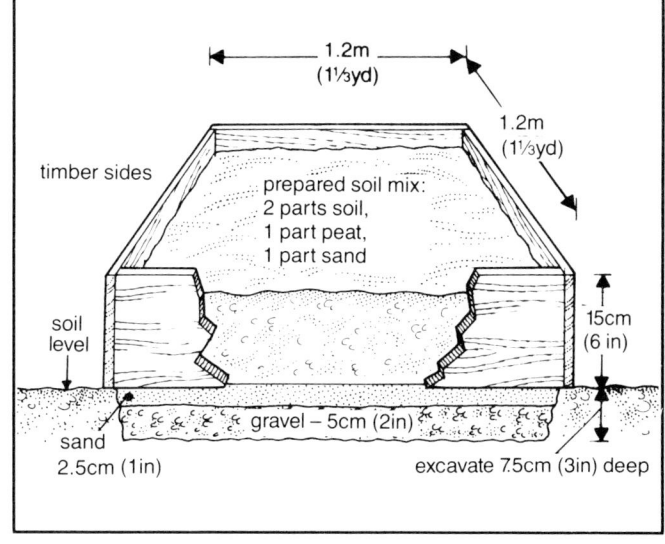

timber sides

prepared soil mix: 2 parts soil, 1 part peat, 1 part sand

1.2m (1⅓yd)

1.2m (1⅓yd)

15cm (6 in)

soil level

sand 2.5cm (1in)

gravel – 5cm (2in)

excavate 7.5cm (3in) deep

PLANNING, PLANTING AND LAYOUT

FIRST THOUGHTS AND PRELIMINARIES

The planning and design process of a garden should start at the earliest opportunity and be an on-going task in conjunction with soil preparation and improvement. Weigh up the site you have available and consider fully the scope for change and development.

One satisfactory approach to garden design is to first decide what is wanted in general terms. This usually consists of a limited allocation of areas for paths, hard surfacing and planting plus any special features. Unfortunately, in the average small modern garden, the freedom of choice is extremely limited and is restricted in the main to the treatment of spaces between paths and walls.

The position of the house and boundaries largely determines the siting of paths and drives. Front gardens tend to be ornamental and decorative in character — they become the shop window dressing and showpiece. Back gardens provide more scope for variety, such as the growing of fruit

The primula family provides many excellent clay soil varieties to give flower colour for most of the year. Displayed here are candelabra primulas.

and vegetables and recreational activities.

Where the modern open-plan style of garden prevails, front boundary fences are not allowed. In such cases, plan and plant in character with the neighbouring gardens to create a pleasing image. This is because each garden becomes a part of what should be a unified landscape and in these circumstances, the most that can be reasonably attempted is a sort of conformist layout featuring the odd tree or shrub and a flower bed or two to break up the lawn or hard surfaced area. In open-plan layouts avoid planting ground-cover and creating pools as both collect litter from far and wide. Pools also act like a magnet to small children, enforcing the need for safety precautions.

Even when front gardens are enclosed, it is better if the design and layout blend in with other gardens nearby. By all means be original in your design, never slavishly copy your neighbours, but don't be obtrusive and cause offence either. Bear in mind security also; don't hide the house completely from view behind excessively high fences or hedges.

Reserve any more exciting and bold planning ideas for the back garden where there is little likelihood of conflict with neighbours. When you plan this area, don't overlook the practicalities. Mention has already been made of giving priority to a sizeable compost area and to providing a hard surfaced sitting area or patio. But what about a coal bunker or oil tank? A clothes drying area needs special consideration too. A rotating clothes drier on concrete is a better bet than a clothes line stretched over the lawn which could cause puddling. Think about installing a toolshed or possibly a greenhouse.

If you have children a play area might be worth considering as it will divert attention from the lawn. All these features need to be incorporated into the overall garden design as unobtrusively as possible without inconvenience or disregard for safety.

Boundaries
When erecting walls and fencing as a demarcation of boundaries, apart from the obvious considerations of screening, privacy and safety,

shelter is of prime importance when gardening on clay. All reasonable measures should be taken to provide shelter and reduce windrock. It is better to go for permeable screens that filter the wind, rather than solid barriers which can cause air turbulence. Try to pay the extra for something which is visually acceptable. Sometimes the height of boundary fences, walls and hedging is kept purposely low, so as not to block exceptional views outside the garden. If this is the case, unless you have a sheltered garden, be content to stick to ground-cover plantings within the garden to minimize wind damage.

Vertical dimensions

There are plenty of candidates for wall coverings on clay soils which when used in conjunction with trellis are safe and effective. Roses, pyracantha and cotoneaster are the first types that spring to mind.

Site assessment and plant growth

Having established that the soil is heavy clay, and the pH value is known, there are other plant habitat factors to consider before full use can be made of the plant lists on pages 74-103.

Find out which parts of the garden are in full sun, part shade and shade. Check areas that are open to early morning sun in spring. Here there are dangers of quick thaws after overnight frosts and resulting damage to opening buds and foliage. Investigate the relative positions of existing trees, hedges, fences, buildings and other structures likely to cast shade. Find out which garden positions are exposed to prevailing winds. If prevailing winds are freezing or drying only the most hardy plants will survive in these conditions.

Discover which are the protected, favoured and sheltered spots suited to the more tender plants. Search out ground contours, noting the direction of the slope, especially if this faces directly towards or away from midday sun. Measure the size of the planting areas; you must bear all these things in mind when choosing plants.

When taking stock of the site, it is also imperative to keep in mind the climate of the district. Pay particular regard to normal maximum and minimum temperatures. These are of special significance when it comes to a plant's hardiness and its ability to survive outdoors all year round.

It is unreasonable to expect plants which originate in the tropical regions to overwinter outdoors in cool climates. The sad outcome is inevitable and nowhere more certain than when gardening on clay soils. Experiment with growing plants of questionable hardiness, and you should always be prepared to take the consequences.

Site assessment is something few people want to dwell on longer than necessary. And in a small garden a brief sketch plan, showing vital measurements and habitat features is all that is necessary for planting purposes.

When considering any new additions or extensions to existing garden layouts, bear in mind the likely present and future labour requirements – don't ignore the initial expenses nor the subsequent running costs.

Exploring possibilities

The next and much more interesting stage of garden design is dreaming up ideas for features to include in any new layout. Obviously, there is greater scope for imagination when starting from scratch in a garden than when updating a partly developed or existing one. One good approach is to make out a list of all the various possible features.

Ornamental rhubarb (rheum) makes a bold accent plant. The large leaves open purple and later turn green. Seek out the red flowered variety R. palmatum 'Rubrum'.

Popular ideas which are particularly relevant to gardens on clay soils are listed on pages 60-4. Examine these ideas one at a time, submitting each one to a number of searching tests:

Appropriateness Does the feature meet personal preferences? Is it in size, scale and, importantly, character with the setting? It would, for example, be inappropriate to random mix bog plants in a severely formal layout.

Colour and interest What is the duration and nature of interest likely to be? For details of individual plants see pages 74-103.

Convenience Is the intended feature practical and suited to the site available? Avoid, for instance, siting a garden pool under trees, this not only makes work as the leaves fall and pollute the water, but also creates undesirable prolonged shade.

Safety Don't plant thorny roses or other prickly hedges beside footpaths, where you run the risk of scratching passers-by. Don't plant heavy topped trees as their spreading branches are likely to be dangerously top-heavy on clay soils. If you have chil-

dren, be wary about planting laburnum, yew and *Arum italicum* – they all flourish on clay but produce poisonous berries or seeds. Also check that water features can be securely grilled and consider covering the greenhouse or conservatory with rigid plastic to avoid injury from breaking glass.

Labour requirements It is very important to strike a good working balance between available labour resources and likely requirements. In short, keep labour-intensive features like roses and annual bedding plants within bounds, unless you are prepared to spend a great deal of time in the garden. Ground cover, once established, and permanent shrub plantings make for labour-saving gardens.

Cost Will expenses be contained to a reasonable affordable level? When laying out a new garden it is very often prudent to carry out the work in stages over several years as this helps to spread the cost as well as the workload. It is, of course, important that the question of running costs should always be kept in mind and layout and features designed to suit your budget accordingly.

Plant suitability In any garden, but with clay soils in particular, it is important to select plants which are suited to the prevailing climatic conditions and which are compatible with the district. Plants which are at home in the habitat are more likely to flourish, and be in keeping with the locality, than when set out in unfavourable surroundings.

Select plants which are clay tolerant and moisture demanding. Other habitat considerations which need to be taken into account are light intensity and shade; the degree of shelter and warmth needed; and the natural water level of the soil (see page 29).

ASSESSMENT OF SPECIAL FEATURES

Hard-surfaced areas
Provided you can afford the initial outlay, if you're uninterested in gardening, or are elderly, disabled or a career person, future hard work can be saved by having the garden professionally hard-landscaped. You can then add as many or as few container plants as you like. These need regular watering and feeding, but are a great deal less work than coping with clay soil, especially if you

are not very interested! Well laid hard surfaces should need minimal maintenance costs to keep them looking good.

Before having a surface laid, make sure you have good foundations (see pages 20-1).

Planting features particularly well suited to clay soils

Flower border There is a wealth of flowering shrubs and herbaceous perennials which flourish on clay soils and collectively give year round colour in the garden. In fact there are few gardens in which a highly satisfactory and pleasing landscape cannot be achieved. General as well as specialist plants can be easily catered for. These are the types which normally give such good value for money, lasting many years before needing replacement. If you choose a wise selection of plants low maintenance of the garden is possible. Flowering shrubs and herbaceous perennials mix satisfactorily to compliment trees, conifers, foliage and annual plants.

Pond and bog garden A garden pond can be developed into a highly desirable special feature. But it is one project which should be left well

alone unless you are prepared to find out how to keep a good balance in the pond life. When plant and animal life are in harmony, the pond will thrive. When they are not, the pool will quickly deteriorate. They involve a fair amount of regular work to clean out and to restock. The initial cost of installing a pool is relatively high, and, as discussed previously, there is always the question of safety with children to consider. The flowering season of pool plants lasts for about ten to twelve weeks during the summer months.

A pool is at its best when it is installed in conjunction with a bog garden to really complete a water garden scene. It is worth considering a rock garden too, but this will obviously add considerably to the initial cost and workload. To do the job properly on clay soils, rock gardens need to be built up over a rubble raft similar to that described for the lawn (see page 20). Once constructed rock gardens enjoy similar advantages to raised garden beds.

A bog garden is normally found by a garden pool, but with little effort on clay soil it is quite feasible to make a bog garden just on its own. It is also a great deal safer if it's a

children's play area. Make use of any of the naturally moist areas in the garden, and if the soil tends to be waterlogged for prolonged periods in winter, plant out on raised mounds. If the area dries out in summer, dig it out to a depth of 23 cm (9 in) and line with a flexible pool liner. Perforate this at intervals to provide weep holes so that any excess water can escape. Make the holes about 15 cm (6 in) below the level of the surrounding soil, assuming that you have a level site. Put rubble on the bottom and top up with good topsoil before planting.

Bog garden plants come in various shapes, sizes and forms, but tend to be bushy, creeping and spiky. Sympathetically handled the resulting varied and informal landscape won't disappoint at all. If you choose plants carefully you can have flowering from early spring until autumn in many vibrant colours with relatively low garden maintenance.

Foliage and fern garden As with the flower garden, there is a wide range of foliage trees, shrubs, conifers, herbaceous perennials and rock plants to choose from. Evergreens are always useful to include to provide varied win-

ter interest. To avoid a stark looking winter, always follow the two to one rule: i.e. plant two evergreen shrubs or trees to each deciduous. A good selection of foliage plants will make excellent ground cover.

Ferns can be happily mixed with the more usual and popularly grown foliage plants. Fern collections are perfect for those cool, shaded moist spots where few other plants are happy to grow. Some will flourish even in very wet conditions. They come in a great variety of form and shape and can be as small as 8 cm (3 in) pygmies to large 2.5 m (8 ft) giants. They can be deciduous or evergreen. These types of plants can be left undisturbed for years without harm and need minimal garden maintenance.

Ferns can also be combined well with woodland and bog plants and look especially good planted with primulas.

Rose garden Roses are particularly linked with clay soils where they will do well provided they are planted in a sunny spot and the soil is deeply worked, well manured and has good drainage.

Large flowered and cluster flowered bush and standard varieties look particularly at home in formal rose beds.

Rodgersia podophylla *is a useful filler for a dull spot. Here it makes a backdrop for bright red candelabra primulas without detracting from their beauty.*

Weeping standards make good specimen plants, whilst dwarf and compact varieties like 'Nozomi' are reasonably good ground-cover. Miniature varieties do well in raised beds and containers, and thornless tall varieties are excellent to create hedging. If you want to screen a wall, fence or archway, grow some ramblers and climbers.

Most people prefer to include the odd rose bed in their garden and leave it at that. But there is obviously scope to create a garden completely full of roses of different varieties. If you want to do this, there is a lot to be said for underbedding and edging. But when doing this, stick to using annual bedding plants, or plants like pansies and violas which can be treated as annuals. This allows for the beds to be cleaned up each autumn and the bushes sprayed in winter.

Apart from its aesthetic value, underbedding also does part of the work of generous mulching. And where mulching materials are in short supply it is well worth trying.

Roses, depending on the variety, will provide beautiful colour and scent for about six months of the year during summer and autumn. They involve a fair amount of work, and expense, in the form of pruning, deadheading and spraying, and supports for standards, climbers and ramblers, but they can be well worth the effort.

Fruit garden Provided that the soil drainage is reasonable, quite a range of fruits will happily thrive on clay soils. Particularly well suited to the soil are culinary tree varieties of apples, plums and damsons. Black currants, gooseberries, blackberries, raspberries and tayberries also do well, but need longer to ripen.

When planting fruit bushes against the walls of buildings, use cordon apples, pears, gooseberries and currants and fan-trained loganberries. Don't be tempted to plant espalier apple, pear, plum and cherry because they make big trees with very active roots which can be a danger causing uneven settlement (see page 117). If intent, however, on growing espaliers grow them against a suitable fence, excluding those with a north or east facing aspect. Make sure you opt for espaliers on dwarfing rootstocks. This is particularly important with apple, pear and cherry. Blackberries and tayberries are at their best on west facing fences where they crop heavily.

SPECIALIST COLLECTORS' PLANTS SUITED TO CLAY SOILS

Initially specialist plant collections are best set out in beds where they can be viewed individually and collectively, and at the same time contribute to the overall effect of the garden. As collections expand and experience is gained, keen garden enthusiasts will develop their own methods for making systematic arrangements.

Astilbe collection

These are good easy plants for a beginner's collection as they can have flower and foliage interest and there are plenty of varieties to choose from. When interplanted with their close relative the golden-leaved *Filipendula ulmaria* 'Aurea', foliage interest from early spring to autumn is assured.

Bog iris collection

As a subject for a plant collection, bog iris are best reserved for the true iris enthusiasts. Attractive as these flowers are they have a relatively brief flowering season of only about six to eight weeks in the summer, from several varieties. Unless relieved by other types of bog plants, bog iris tend to be rather stiff and formal in appearance and lack interest for much of the year. Take care to choose moisture-loving varieties because the iris family includes many members which need well-drained soils.

Half-hardy chrysanthemum collection

These are primarily for the exhibitor and flower arranger, not the average collector. They offer great variation in shape and form, but it has to be stressed that although moist root conditions are required, so is good drainage. The plants should be lifted out of the soil annually and moved under cover for the winter months. Here they can be used as stock plants for propagation purposes, so that young plants can be raised and then set out each spring. Chrysanthemums are hard work, not only with regard to propagation, but also with the spraying and subsequent supporting which is always necessary for these plants.

Dahlia collection

These are hard work like half-hardy chrysanthemums. They are specialist flowers for the avid exhibitor and flower arranger. However, there is more scope for using collections for garden decoration and indeed they can be very showy. They again need good drainage and come in a great variety of flowers. Dahlias are labour intensive if the tubers are overwintered and the plants home raised. They need staking, tying and spraying, plus generous feeding.

Hemerocallis (day lily) collection

These flowers are increasing in popularity for specialist collections with a succession of varieties providing spectacular colour displays for 8 to 10 weeks in the summer months. Collections are easier than most to fit into the average garden since they can be grouped by height, colour and flowering times.

Hosta (plantain lily) collection

This is a good foliage collection to start with. They are un-beatable foliage plants and provide outstanding bold effects from late spring to autumn, but you do need to allow adequate space.

Paeony collection

Each season there is an increase in the popularity of the paeony as a collector's plant. This is another good plant for the beginner, but like hostas needs to be given space. The chief drawback is their relatively short flowering season which lasts from May to July.

Primula collection

An interesting and varied colourful collection of hardy primulas can be contained in a small space. They are among the best of collector's plants.

PLANTING

The plants

When selecting plants to set out on heavy clay, it cannot be recommended too strongly to make the choice first and foremost on an ecological basis. This means choosing plants which are well suited to the available site, soil and climate.

If you do choose plants which are just not suitable for clay soils, such as carnations and pinks which thrive in light sandy soil, there are likely to be two consequences. Firstly, the plants soon be-come unhealthy, and secondly a great deal of unsuccessful time, money and effort will have been spent trying to alter the environment to suit the plants.

Rootstocks and pollination
Check with your supplier that budded or grafted trees are on suitable rootstocks. Generally speaking the more dwarfing the rootstocks are the better. Rootstocks are of increasing importance on clay because, once established, trees on vigorous rootstocks are likely to grow far too big. With fruit trees don't overlook the ques-

tion of pollinator varieties either with special regard to flowering times. On clay lush leaves tend to be produced at the expense of flowers. And since flowers are sparse a full fruit set is needed if a decent crop is to be harvested. A full fruit set will only be achieved if pollinator and pollinated varieties are in close proximity to each other and flower at the same time. There is no need to worry, however, with self-fertile varieties, or with family trees where two or three compatible varieties are worked onto one rootstock.

Plant condition The golden rule when buying plants to set out on clay soils is to go for those which are well grown, sturdy and grown in *containers*. This goes for trees, shrubs climbers, herbaceous perennials and rock plants as well as half-hardy annuals. Plants then have the best chance of breaking out into the clay soil without severe setback. Don't buy plants which are pot bound and have obviously been left around for some time. Also remember to steer clear of bare-root plants with the possible exception of rose bushes for autumn planting. However, autumn planting of roses should only be attempted in sheltered gardens and favoured sites where the soil is well worked, well drained and very fertile.

Make sure that all indoor raised plants are suitably hardened off and acclimatized before setting out in the garden, again to minimize setback.

When to plant
Planting times on clay soils must be geared as much or more to the state of the soil as to the month, climate and variety. Again remember never to plant when the soil is wet, frozen or baked hard.

In cold exposed sites where the soil tends to remain waterlogged for long periods in winter any intention of autumn planting of trees and shrubs, including conifers, is best forgotten. Wait until the spring, and even then don't be in a rush.

With a similar climate planting in spring is usually later on clay soils than on light sandy loams. This is because clay soils are slower to warm up and temperature becomes a major factor. For hardy trees, shrubs and herbaceous perennials it is normal to wait until the soil has warmed up and reached a temperature of around 5°C (41°F). Experienced gardening hands can gauge the soil temperature and until such time as this becomes second nature, don't be afraid to buy a soil thermometer and use that.

The popular advice of planting spring flowering herbaceous perennials in the autumn should be ignored when gardening on clay, unless you have good soil drainage and the condition of the soil is well above average. Autumn planted spring bedding is a bit of a gamble too, and is best deferred for a few years until the soil is well broken in. The same applies to spring flowering bulbs.

In the interim, in mild areas, all spring bedding and bulbs will grow satisfactorily in display containers. They do particularly well if they are placed in the shelter of the patio.

How to plant

Pay careful attention to detail when planting on clay, it makes all the difference between ultimate success and failure. The most common failings among gardeners are:

1 Bad siting in the garden with plants left exposed to cold and strong winds, invariably leading to an unacceptable level of disturbance from the wind with water collecting around the necks of plants. Rotting and disease will soon follow.

2 Planting at the wrong depth. With clay soils the usual fault is to plant too deep. Remember to keep the crowns well up when planting herbaceous perennials. This point is especially important when planting flowers like paeonies.

3 Bad planting practices. One of the most damaging faults is to overfirm and cramp the roots.

4 Inadequate staking. Once established on clay plants tend to produce many leaves and are inclined to be top-heavy with a great dependance on staking and tying. Don't make ties too tight on permanent plants and allow for some movement at the roots.

5 Poor soil preparations, see pages 36-48.

6 Poor aftercare, see pages 104-111.

Planting trees and shrubs

As a general rule, don't plant any tree closer to a building than a distance equal to its ultimate height. However, with vigorous rooting trees like willow, oak, poplar and sycamore you will need to double this distance, or better still select alternative varieties. The fact that clay soils expand on wetting and shrink on drying does not seriously damage buildings or their foundations, provided the expansion and contraction is uniform around the building. But the moment tree roots are involved, which remove vast amounts of water, differential rates of expansion and contraction begin. This results in many structural problems – uneven settlement, damaged foundations and cracked walls letting in damp and frost. Added to this must be the direct damage from tree roots which happens to any soil. Roots find their way into small cracks in foundations and as they grow they force the cracks to enlarge.

In a recent survey of tree damage to buildings due to root action it is a sobering thought that 88% of the cases occurred on clay soils. Similar problems with root damage arise when trees are planted too near to underground drains and mains services.

Following the above planting distances to their logical conclusion would suggest excluding trees from many small gardens altogether. One practical and popular answer if you are a tree lover is to grow trees in containers. Another alternative is to grow them in tree boxes to restrict the root growth. This allows trees to be grown relatively close to buildings and services with the minimum

risk of damage. But you do need to choose less vigorous varieties when you do intend to use tree boxes.

Tree box construction Dig out a hole about 1.2 m (4 ft) square and 90 cm (3 ft) deep, in a position where there is no risk of interfering with underground services and stack the topsoil neatly to one side. Consolidate a 10 cm (4 in) layer of rubble in the bottom, then lay a 7.5 cm (3 in) thick and 30 cm (12 in) wide bed of concrete around the outer edge of the rubble raft. Using the concrete as the foundation, line the sides of the hole with a single-course brick

Fig. 7. Grow trees in tree boxes where there is a risk of root damage to building foundations.

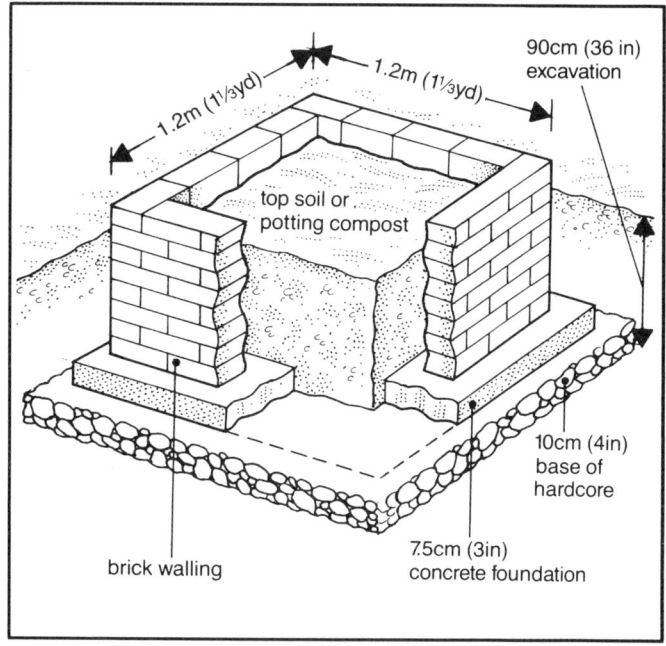

90cm (36 in) excavation

1.2m (1⅓yd)

1.2m (1⅓yd)

top soil or potting compost

10cm (4in) base of hardcore

brick walling

7.5cm (3in) concrete foundation

For those with plenty of space, a bed of mixed hostas is unbeatable for foliage display. Very often there is a bonus show of flowers.

wall to form a square bottomless box.

The top of the box should be slightly above the surrounding soil or paving. Fill the completed box with good topsoil and plant the tree in a pocket of planting mixture, see page 72.

Raised beds Although a more sophisticated version, the idea here is the same as for a raised seed bed (see page 70) to build a bed of good topsoil above the general level of the surrounding soil. Raised beds are of particular value where the soil is low lying and wet, and where the fertility is low. Some permanent planting can be undertaken in a raised bed while the soil in the remainder of

the garden is gradually fertilized and improved. Of course raised beds can make an attractive feature in their own right, providing height and change of level, but they are not necessarily a remedial feature.

Relate the size of bed to planting. A 90 cm (3 ft) square is a useful size – to take a single large tree, a group of three small trees or shrubs, a collection of miniature roses, or a number of herbaceous perennials. Aim for walls about 30 cm (12 in) above the surrounding border. Those of simulated stone, brick, concrete blocks or paving slabs are all satisfactory. Well-preserved timber is quick to erect, but rots in time when backed with wet soil.

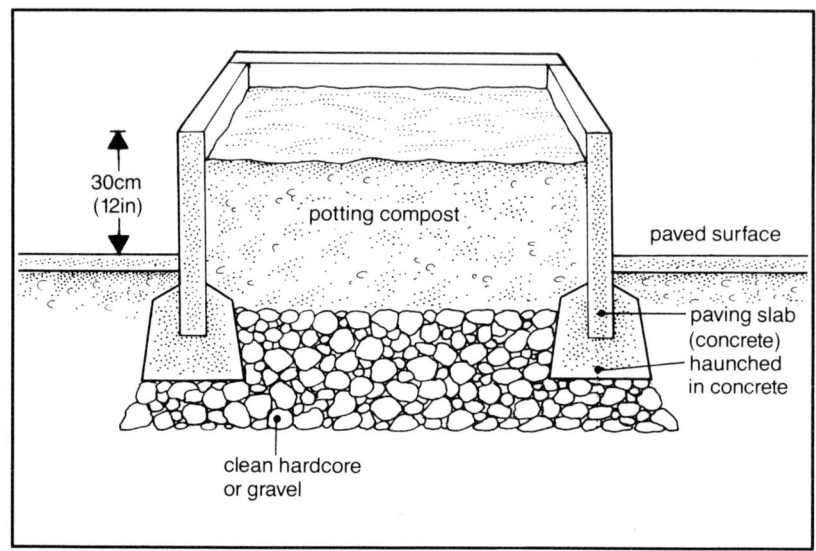

Fig. 8.   Where the garden soil is infertile, build a bed of good topsoil to successfully grow ornamental plants and vegetables.

30cm (12in)

potting compost

paved surface

paving slab (concrete) haunched in concrete

clean hardcore or gravel

It is imperative that the walling is set on a sound foundation. The depth of top-soil should not be less than about 60 cm (24 in) for trees, slightly less for shrubs, and about 25 cm (10 in) will suffice for herbaceous perennials. For trees excavate out the raised bed area to a little over 75 cm (2 ft) deep to allow for rubble and concrete foundations similar to the tree box, page 69. Adjust the depth in proportion to suit the other plantings.

Preparation of planting pockets Regardless of planting into tree boxes, raised beds, the border, the lawn, or into paved areas where the odd paving slab has been lifted, garden trees and shrubs really are best planted out into pockets of well prepared soil.

Dig out planting pockets at least double the rootball width and half as deep again as the container. Loosen the bottom and sides of the hole with a garden fork as this helps to relieve compaction and encourages roots to grow into the surrounding soil more quickly. Fork plenty of peat, well rotted manure or garden compost and some bonemeal into the bottom of the pocket. Cover the bottom with about 5 cm (2 in) of

planting mix – a good mixture consists of one part each of sand and peat with three parts good topsoil (imported if need be). Mix in a small handful each of bonemeal and general fertilizer to each bucketful of mix.

If the trees have been raised in peat-based potting composts then make up the planting mixture with two parts each of peat and topsoil and one part of sand. This makes the transition to heavy clay soil more gradual and easier for the plant to cope with.

Stakes are best hammered home before planting out, so avoiding possible damage to tree roots (see page 106).

Planting Thoroughly soak the rootball with water and allow the container to drain for at least an hour before disturbing the plant. If, on removing the container the roots are in any way matted, gently tease out some of the outer ones, and uncoil any long roots at the base, trimming back any which are damaged. Position the tree in the hole, setting it at the same depth as before the move. Gently firm planting mix between the roots and the sides of the pocket to fill up level with the surface. At the surface it is important to dome the soil away from the trunk slightly.

Potting trees and shrubs in containers Pot trees and shrubs into containers 5-8 cm (2-3 in) larger in diameter than the previous container. Position large containers in their permanent resting places before filling. And unless raised up on legs, stand them on a level gravel bed for good drainage. Cover the drainage holes with gauze, add clean pebbles, covering these with damp peat and then add a layer of planting mixture. In containers it is best to use strong soil-based potting compost like John Innes No 3 for long term planting. Fill and firm the soil in containers as described above for planting pockets.

Planting wall plants and climbers Set them in planting pockets 30 cm (12 in) out from the wall. Don't tie them in too tightly at the base so as to allow for soil settlement and movement.

Planting hedges and edges Plant these out on a raised ridge over a prepared trench (see page 51).

Planting alpines and rock plants Dig out the heavy clay soil and replace with some pockets of soil-based potting compost, topdress with grit after planting.

Planting border perennials in beds, borders and bog gardens With this type of planting it pays to take out generous sized pockets. Work planting mix in and around the roots and then around the plants after planting. Generally speaking, it is advisable to set the plants slightly less deeply than normal. If the soil is wet raise them up on mounds.

Planting pool plants Plant these in hessian-lined aquatic baskets, using organic free loam and following the guidelines on labels in connection with depth and spacing.

Planting bedding plants and vegetables Buy young seedling plants and pot them up singly into small pots with potting compost. Plants are then set out with a good rootball and stand a reasonable chance of growing without setback.

Planting herbs With heavy soil, herbs, with the possible exception of mint, are really best grown in containers of free-draining compost. Stand containers in a sunny spot, near the house.

TREES AND CONIFERS FOR CLAY SOILS

Although many broad-leaved trees and conifers do grow successfully on clay soils, don't expect them to tolerate either waterlogged soil conditions or just plain neglect. Good soil preparation is essential and not to be forgotten.

It is folly to plant forest trees in small gardens for quick effect when their roots are known to cause serious damage to nearby buildings, structures, drains and services. This is particularly true of clay soils (see page 68). A selection of small to medium-sized tree varieties, which can be planted without undue risk in an average modern garden, is to be found in the following pages.

Container trees

The choice of trees for container growing is, of course, not limited to clay tolerance. But for ease of management and aftercare it is wise to restrict the selection to small, less vigorous, hardy varieties. It is also just as important to bear in mind prevailing site conditions in the same way as you would when selecting trees to plant direct.

Euonymus is a good safe evergreen shrub for most soils. The surrounding plants above will only grow over clay if the soil is drastically modified.

Plant naming

When buying garden trees it is very important to get the full name correct. Most garden plants have two names: the first is the Latin or botanical which is recognized internationally; the second is the popular or local name. The botanical name is normally made up of two or three parts: The first part (the surname if you like) is the genus or generic name, the second part is the species or specific name, which can be likened to a Christian or first name, the third part is the varietal name – a further sub-division of the species. For example:

Acer negundo 'Variegatum': *Acer* is the genus – the surname *negundo* is the species – the Christian name 'Variegatum' is the variety, a special selection of negundo.

QUICK GUIDE – CONIFERS FOR CLAY

Genus	Popular name
Abies	Fir
Chamaecyparis	Cypress
Juniperus	Juniper
Picea	Spruce
Taxus	Yew
Thuja	Arbor vitae

QUICK GUIDE – BROAD-LEAVED TREES FOR CLAY

Genus	Popular name	Genus	Popular name
Acer	Maple	Malus	Crab apple
Arbutus	Strawberry tree	Prunus	Cherry, plum
		Pyrus	Pear
Alnus	Alder	Salix	Willow
Amelanchier	Snowy Mespilus	Sorbus	Rowan and whitebeam
Betula	Birch	Syringa	Lilac
Carpinus	Hornbeam	Tamarix	Tamarisk
Cornus	Cornelian cherry		
Cotoneaster	Cotoneaster		
Crataegus	Thorn or May		
Ilex	Holly		
Laburnum	Laburnum		

BROAD-LEAVED TREES FOR CLAY – DESCRIPTIVE GUIDE

Acer Maple. Deciduous, foliage effects.
A. ginnala – Amur maple; **A. griseum** – Paperbark maple; **A. negundo** 'Variegatum' – Variegated box elder.
Pruning Negligible, but always remove suckers on sight.

Arbutus Strawberry tree. Strawberry-like fruits and flowers appear together in late autumn. Evergreen.
A. unedo – white flowers; **A. u.** 'Rubra' – pink flowers.
Pruning Minimal apart from trimming to shape in late spring.
Problems Not reliably hardy in cold areas.

Alnus Alder. Attractive shiny deciduous leaves and persistent catkins.
A. incana 'Aurea' – red-tinted yellow catkins and bright orange bark.
Pruning Minimal. Clip hedges of **A. incana** 'Aurea' in late spring.

Amelanchier Mespilus. Attractive white spring flowers, summer fruits and eyecatching deciduous foliage.
A. lamarckii – certainly won't disappoint.
Pruning Thin out overcrowded shoots in autumn in alternate years.

Problems Not suitable for lime rich soils.

Betula Birch. Deciduous with yellow autumn leaf tints. Trunks outstanding.
B. pendula 'Youngii' – Young's weeping birch. One of the best for confined spaces.
Pruning Occasionally thin out branches in autumn.
Problems Many grow too big for small gardens. Sometimes attacked by leaf-eating pests.

Carpinus Hornbeam (see page 87).

Cornus Dogwoods. Coloured bark and attractive deciduous foliage.
C. mas – Cornelian cherry. Tiny yellow late winter flowers, bronze-red autumn leaf tints and red fruits.
Pruning Minimal
Problems Not for cold exposed gardens.

Cotoneaster White summer flowers and a profusion of autumn berries.
C. 'Cornubia' – semi-evergreen bushy tree; **C. hybridus** 'Pendulus' – semi-evergreen/evergreen of stiffly weeping habit.
Pruning Thin out badly placed shoots in summer and prune to shape.

Crataegus Hawthorn. Late spring flowers, autumn berries and attractive deciduous summer foliage, some have autumn tints.

C. oxyacantha 'Coccinea Plena' – Paul's double scarlet thorn; *C. o.* 'Plena'; *C. prunifolia* – Plum-leaved thorn.

Pruning Thin out overcrowded shoots and prune to shape in autumn or winter.

Problems Occasionally attacked by boring pests, sometimes infected by mildew.

Ilex Holly (see page 88).

Laburnum Golden chains. Deciduous with a profusion of long, graceful pendulous flower racemes in late spring or early summer.

L. anagyroides – Common laburnum; *L.* x *watereri* 'Vossii'.

Pruning Shorten misplaced shoots in summer.

Problems In autumn the pods contain poisonous seeds. Leaf blotch miner occasionally attacks.

Malus Ornamental crab. Deciduous flowering and fruiting trees.

M. 'John Downie' – pink-budded white flowers, orange red fruits; *M.* 'Royalty' – pink flowers, wine-red fruits, glossy purple foliage; *M. sargentii* – the smallest crab, white flowers and currant-like red fruits.

Pruning Thin out overcrowded and misplaced shoots in autumn.

Problems Aphids, caterpillars, mildew and scab sometimes cause concern.

Prunus Cherry, plum. Stick to flowering plums or Japanese cherries on clay soils. Deciduous.

P. cerasifera 'Nigra' – pink spring flowers, blackish-purple stems and summer foliage; *P. c.* 'Pissardii' – white blossom, wine-red foliage; *P. c.* 'Rosea' – pink blossom, bronze-purple spring foliage.

Pruning Shorten straggly shoots in late summer or early autumn.

Pyrus Ornamental pears. Attractive deciduous autumn tinted foliage and white spring blossom.

P. calleryana 'Chanticleer' – Chinese pear; *P. communis* 'Beech Hill' – Wild pear; *P. salicifolia* 'Pendula' – Weeping willow-leaved pear.

Pruning Occasionally thin out misplaced shoots and overcrowded branches in autumn.

Problems Caterpillars and mildew may attack.

Salix Willow. Attractive deciduous foliage and abundant catkins.

S. caprea 'Pendula' – Kilmarnock willow, stiffly downswept stems, pussy willow catkins in late winter; *S. purpurea* 'Pendula' – Purple weeping willow, weeping purple-tinged branches.

Although visually attractive, growing euonymus through berberis on clay soils is to invite die-back on the berberis and revertion on the euonymus. Not for beginners.

Pruning Minimal

Problems Most willows grow too big and are notorious for root damage to foundations, so select the above varieties. Caterpillars can be a nuisance and keep a careful eye open for anthracnose, a disease which spoils foliage appearance.

Sorbus Mountain ash. Deciduous with ivory white or pink early summer flower clusters, masses of yellow or red late summer or autumn berries and often autumn leaf tints.

S. aucuparia – Rowan or Mountain ash; *S. aucuparia 'Xanthocarpa'; S. cashmiriana; S. sargentiana.*

Pruning Minimal

Problems Red berried varieties are often stripped by birds.

Syringa Lilac. Deciduous with large clusters of tiny single or double scented spring/early summer flowers. *S.* 'Charles Joly' – purplish-red double flowers; *S.* 'Edward J. Gardner' – large pink flower heads; *S.* 'Firmament' – sky-blue single flowers; *S.* 'Katherine Havemeyer' – purple-lavender double flowers; *S.* 'Maud Notcutt' – white; *S.* 'Souvenir de Lonis Spaeth' – wine-red.

Pruning Remove flower buds in first season after planting and deadhead in early years, minimal pruning needed thereafter.

Tamarix Tamarisk. Feathery green foliage and pink flowers.

T. gallica – Common tamarisk, evergreen in mild districts, deciduous in cold areas.

Pruning Deadhead young trees. Shorten back frosted tips in spring.

CONIFERS FOR CLAY –DESCRIPTIVE GUIDE

Abies Silver firs. Evergreen conifers.

A. koreana Korean fir. Shiny dark-green needles with silver reverse, bright pink-crimson spring flowers, purple-blue/violet autumn cones. Named varieties are less suited to clay soils than the species.

Pruning Normally unnecessary.

Chamaecyparis Cypress. Varieties of Lawson cypress are best suited to clay soil. Flattened fan-like evergreen branchlets of green or variegated foliage.

Tall C. lawsoniana-blue-green; *C. l.* 'Columnaris Glauca'; *C. l.* 'Pembury Blue'-blue; *C. l.* 'Stewartii Erecta' – bright yellow.

Small C. lawsoniana

'Ellwoodii' – feathery blue-green; *C. l.* 'Ellwood's Gold' – gold-tipped branchlets.

Pruning Fell tall varieties after 12 years or they will grow too big. Clip tall hedging twice a year to contain at 3 m (10 ft). Otherwise minimal.

Juniperus Junipers.
J. communis 'Hibernica' – Irish juniper, one of the very best garden trees. Neat pyramidal habit, attractive blue-green foliage.
Pruning Minimal.

Picea Spruce.
P. glauca 'Albertiana Conica' – a dwarf, evergreen cone of green grass-like foliage reaching 75 cm (2½ ft) in ten years.
Pruning Unnecessary.
Problems Red spider likely to attack in prolonged hot dry weather. Most spruces grow too large.

Taxus Yew. Slow growing evergreens with green or variegated foliage.
T. baccata 'Fastigiata' – Irish yew, a compact narrow dark green column; *T. b.* 'Standishii'-yellow foliage.
Pruning Unnecessary.
Problems Scale insects can attack. Foliage and berries poisonous.

Thuja Arborvitae. Flattened sprays of evergreen foliage.
T. occidentalis 'Holmstrup' – a narrow bright green column; *T. o.* 'Rheingold' – a dwarf with gold summer foliage tinted coppery in winter; *T. o.* 'Smaragd' – an emerald green column.
Pruning Unnecessary.
Problems Thuja blight.

SHRUBS AND CLIMBERS FOR CLAY SOILS

HINTS AND TIPS

Shrub selection

When buying shrubs and climbers for clay soils it is equally as important as with trees to check the name fully (see page 76).

Container plants

Again as with trees, the choice of shrubs and climbers for growing in containers is not restricted to clay tolerance, and opens up numerous and exciting alternative possibilities.

Drainage

At the risk of repetition, suitability of shrubs and climbers to heavy clay soils does not imply tolerance of waterlogging. Rather, drainage improvement and good soil preparations on the part of the gardener are assumed.

Use shrubs effectively

As an aid to plant selection, the following 'At-a-Glance Guide' lists shrubs and climbers suitable for clay soils, together with some ideas for special uses. Further details of individual plants are given in the 'Descriptive Guide' which is included in the following pages.

Loosetrife (lysimachia) can make an attractive border or waterside plant. But it is important to plant in scale with the surroundings – opt for dwarf varieties.

KEY TO AT-A-GLANCE GUIDE

Key to At-A-Glance Guide
Main Uses
0 = Cut flower arranging
1 = Border shrub
2 = Climber or wall plant
3 = Ground cover
4 = Hedging or edging
5 = Free-standing accent or specimen plant
6 = Container plant

AT-A-GLANCE GUIDE – SHRUBS AND CLIMBERS FOR HEAVY SOILS

Botanical name	Popular name	Uses						
		0	1	2	3	4	5	6
Aucuba	Aucuba	+	+	−	−	−	−	−
Berberis	Barberry	+	+	−	+	+	+	+
Buxus	Box	+	+	−	−	+	+	+
Carpinus	Hornbeam	−	−	−	−	+	−	−
Chaenomeles	Flowering quince	+	+	+	−	+	−	+
Choisya	Mexican orange	+	+	+	−	−	+	+
Clematis	Virgins bower	−	−	+	−	−	−	−
Cornus	Dogwood	+	+	−	−	−	+	−
Cotoneaster	Cotoneaster	+	+	+	+	+	+	+
Crataegus	Thorn	−	−	−	−	+	−	−
Deutzia	Deutzia	+	+	−	+	+	−	+
Elaeagnus	Oleaster	+	+	−	−	+	+	+
Euonymus	Spindle	+	+	+	+	+	+	+
Forsythia	Golden bell bush	+	+	+	−	+	+	+
Fuchsia	Ladies eardrops	+	+	+	−	+	+	+
Hedera	Ivy	+	−	+	+	−	−	+
Hypericum	St John's wort	+	+	−	+	+	−	+
Ilex	Holly	−	+	−	−	+	+	+
Jasminum	Jasmine	+	−	+	−	−	−	+
Kerria	Kerria	+	+	+	−	−	−	+
Ligustrum	Privet	+	+	−	−	+	+	+
Mahonia	Oregon grape	+	+	−	+	+	+	+
Philadelphus	Mock orange	+	+	−	−	−	+	−
Prunus	Laurel	+	+	−	+	+	−	+
Pyracantha	Firethorn	+	+	+	−	+	+	−
Rhododendron & azalea	Rhododendron & azalea	−	+	−	+	+	+	+
Ribes	Flowering currant	+	+	−	−	+	+	+
Rosa	Rose	+	+	+	+	+	+	+
Sambucus	Elder	+	+	−	−	−	+	−
Spiraea	Spiraea	+	+	−	+	−	+	+
Symphoricarpus	Snowberry	+	+	−	−	+	−	−
Syringa	Lilac	+	+	−	−	−	+	+
Tamarix	Tamarisk	+	+	−	−	+	+	+
Viburnum	Guelder rose	+	+	+	+	+	+	+
Vinca	Periwinkle	+	+	−	+	+	−	+

AT-A-GLANCE GUIDE – SHRUBS AND CLIMBERS FOR HEAVY SOILS

Botanical Name	Popular Name	Uses						
		0	1	2	3	4	5	6
Weigela	Weigela	+		−	−	−	+	+
Conifers			+					
Chamaecyparis	Cypress	−	+	−	+	+	+	+
Taxus	Yew	−	+	−	−	+	+	+

SHRUBS AND CLIMBERS FOR CLAY DESCRIPTIVE GUIDE

Aucuba Spotted/variegated laurel. Large, bold, glossy evergreen leaves are usually leathery and green with gold variegation. Bright scarlet winter berries on female plants. Soot and pollution tolerant.
A. japonica 'Gold Dust'; **A. japonica** 'Picturata'; **A. japonica** 'Salicifolia'.
Pruning Negligible.

Berberis Barberry. Renowned for prickles and sharp spines.
Deciduous varieties – interesting foliage in spring and autumn, yellow spring flowers, pink, red or crimson berries. **B. thunbergii atropurpurea; B. t.** 'Atropurpurea Nana'; **B. wilsonae.**
Evergreen varieties – glossy dark green leaves, yel-low, orange or crimson tinted flowers, muted blue-black berries. **B. candidula; B. darwinii; B.** x **stenophylla.**
Pruning For formal effects and hedging clip regularly to shape in summer. Otherwise prune deciduous kinds in autumn; evergreens in summer.
Problems Look for aphids and rust.

Buxus Box. Dense, green or variegated evergreen aromatic foliage.
B. sempervirens – Common box, green leaved; **B. s.** 'Suffruticosa' – Edging box, a glossy dark green dwarf.
Pruning Clip as necessary in late spring or summer.

Carpinus Hornbeam. Deciduous but leaves persist well into winter in a dried state.
C. betulus – Common hornbeam.
Pruning Clip in late summer/early autumn to restrain as hedging.

Chaenomeles Flowering quince. Flower buds which are giant, apple-blossom-like in red, pink or white, open on bare branches in late winter – mature plants carry golden quinces in late autumn.
Tall varieties: C. speciosa 'Cardinalis', red; **C. speciosa** 'Nivalis', white; **C. speciosa** 'Umbilicata', pink.
Bush varieties: C. x superba 'Pink Lady', pink; **C.** x s. 'Rowallane', red.
Pruning Shorten long new growths in summer.

Choisya Mexican orange. Scented glossy evergreen leaves and fragrant white spring flowers.
C. ternata, dark green leaves; **C. t.** 'Sundance', golden leaves.
Pruning Shorten straggly growths, frosted tips and overcrowded shoots in late spring.
Problems Not reliably hardy outside mild areas.

Clematis Showy, flowering climbers. On heavy soil stick to deciduous varieties like:–
C. x 'Jackmanii Superba', violet purple; **C.** 'Nelly Moser', pink striped blush white; **C.** 'The President', purple; **C.** 'Ville de Lyon', carmine-red; **C. montana,** white; **C. m. rubens** rose.
Pruning Consult a reputable catalogue.
Problems Look out for clematis wilt.

Cornus Dogwood. Coloured winter stems, attractive deciduous foliage, autumn leaf tints.
Red stemmed: C. alba 'Sibirica'; **C. alba** 'Spaethii'.
Yellow stemmed: C. stolonifera 'Flaviramea'.
Pruning For best stem colour cut back annually in late winter to 10 cm (4 in) above ground.

Cotoneaster White summer flowers, red or orange autumn berries.
Evergreen: C. 'Skogholm Coral Beauty'; **C. lacteus.**
Deciduous: C. horizontalis.
Pruning Minimal
Problems Berry eating birds and aphid infestations.

Crataegus Hawthorn (see pages 77-8).
Grow **C. oxyacantha** varieties and **C. monogyna** quickthorn – as shrubs.
Pruning Thin out bushes, clip formal specimens/hedging in autumn.

Deutzia Abundance of white or pink summer flowers. Deciduous.
D. x **elegantissima; D.** x 'Mont Rose'; **D.** x rosea; **D.** scabra 'Pride of Rochester'.
Pruning Thin out weak branches and oldest flowered shoots after flowering.
Problems Generally trouble-free.

Leopard plants are strong growers and can quickly outgrow their allotted space on clay soil – stick to less vigorous varieties like Ligularia clivorum 'Desdemona'.

Elaeagnus Oleaster. Evergreen foliage shrubs.
E. pungens 'Maculata' – outstanding variety.
Pruning Shorten straggly shoots, clip formal specimens in early summer.

Euonymus Evergreen spindle. Pollution tolerant foliage shrubs.
E. fortunei 'Colorata' – purplish-green climber; **E. f.** 'Emerald 'n' Gold' – golden variegated hummock; **E. japonicus** – green; **E. japonicus** 'Aureopictus' – golden variegated.
Pruning Clip to shape in summer. Tie in climbers.

Forsythia Golden Bell Bush. Bright yellow spring flowers. Deciduous.
F. 'Lynwood'; **F. suspensa.**
Pruning Thin out or clip in summer.

Fuchsia Ladies eardrops. Summer and autumn flowers in pinks, purples, reds and white. Deciduous.
F. 'Riccartonii' – scarlet-purple; **F.** 'Tom Thumb' – dwarf violet-carmine.
Pruning In mild areas shorten shoots back by a third in early spring, elsewhere cut down to almost ground level.

Hedera Ivy. Evergreen, self clinging foliage climbers.
H. helix 'Buttercup'; **H. h.** 'Chicago Variegata'; **H. h.** 'Glacier'; **H. h.** 'Goldheart'.
Pruning Clip straggly side growths in spring and summer and stop main shoots when necessary.
Problems Look out for scale insects. Train over trellis or risk damage to brickwork.

Hypericum St John's wort. Large yellow summer flowers; red, orange or black autumn seed pods. Autumn leaf tints on deciduous kinds.
H. calycinum – Rose of Sharon, evergreen; **H. forrestii,** deciduous; **H.** 'Hidcote', deciduous.
Pruning Shorten back in late winter or spring.

Ilex Holly. Evergreen green or variegated prickly, red-berried foliage shrubs.
I. x altaclarensis 'Golden King'; **I. aquifolium** 'J. C. van Tol'; **I. a.** 'Argentea Marginata'; **I. a.** 'Golden Milkboy'; **I. a.** 'Pyramidalis'.
Pruning Clip to shape in summer. Cut out green shoots on variegated kinds.
Problems Look for leaf mining maggot. Not all varieties have berries.

Jasminum Jasmine. White or yellow flowered wall plants. Stick to deciduous varieties on clay.
J. nudiflorum – Winter jasmine; **J. officinale** 'Grandiflorum' – Common jasmine.

Pruning Cut back almost to main framework after flowering.
Problems Common jasmine is subject to blackfly.

Kerria Grow *K. japonica* 'Pleniflora' on clay – deciduous, yellow flowered and green stemmed.
Pruning Cut out the oldest flowered stems after blooming in spring.

Ligustrum Privet. Quick growing green or variegated foliage shrubs with whitish scented summer flowers. Semi-evergreen – deciduous in cold areas.
L. ovalifolium – Oval-leaf privet; *L. ovalifolium* 'Aureum' – Golden privet.
Pruning Clip as required in summer, do so frequently for formal hedging.

Mahonia includes Oregon grape. Evergreen foliage, yellow scented flowers, blue-black berried, shrubs.
M. aquifolium – Oregon grape; *M. a.* 'Atropurpurea'; *M.* x 'Charity'.
Pruning Cut out a quarter of the oldest shoots in late spring or early summer.

Philadelphus Mock orange. Strongly scented, creamy-white summer flowers. Deciduous.
P. 'Sybille' and *P.* 'Virginal' are best for clay.

Pruning Cut out weak and spent flower shoots in summer after blooming.
Problems Blackfly infestations.

Prunus Laurel. Evergreen, pollution tolerant, shiny leaved foliage shrub. Has white spring flowers and red autumn berries.
P. laurocerasus – Common laurel; *P. laurocerasus* 'Otto Luyken'.
Pruning Shape with secateurs in late summer.

Pyracantha Firethorn. Evergreen with ivory summer flowers and brilliant red, orange or yellow autumn/winter berries.
P. rogersiana – red berries; *P. r.* 'Flava' – yellow berries.
Pruning Shorten soft new shoots to shape in summer.
Problems Subject to aphid attack and fireblight disease.

Rhododendron Rhododendrons/azaleas. Stick to evergreen *R. yakushimanum* hybrids on clay – brilliant late spring flowers. Soil must be well prepared and heavily mulched.
Pruning Nil apart from deadheading young plants.
Problems Weevils can attack. Look for chlorosis if soil is limy or water hard.

Ribes Flowering currant. Deciduous with pendulous

clusters of white, pink or red spring flowers amongst opening leaves.

R. sanguineum 'Brocklebankii' – pink; ***R. s.*** 'Pulborough Scarlet'; ***R. s.*** 'Tydeman's White'.

Pruning After flowering shorten back the new shoots by half and then thin out old wood.

Rosa Roses. Stick to modern varieties of climbers, ramblers, large flowered, cluster-flowered miniatures and shrub roses.

Consult a good up to date catalogue for details of varieties.

Pruning Consult a good rose book.

Problems Many pests and diseases get a hold unless sprayed regularly.

Sambucus Elderberry. Grow ***S. nigra*** 'Aurea', Golden elder on clay. Large clusters of white spring flowers, black autumn fruits.

Pruning Shorten main stems to shape in autumn.

Spiraea Stick to summer flowering varieties with coloured or variegated leaves. ***S. x bumalda*** 'Anthony Waterer' and ***S. x b.*** 'Goldflame' are both crimson flowered.

Pruning Cut down to 10 cm (4 in) above ground in the late winter.

Symphoricarpus Snowberry. Deciduous with glistening white, pink, crimson or purple rounded autumn/winter berries.

S. rivularis 'Common snowberry, white; ***S. x doorenbosii*** 'Magic Berry' lilac-crimson-carmine; ***S. x d.*** 'Mother of Pearl', white-tinged-pink.

Pruning Thin out weak and overcrowded shoots in late winter. Remove suckers.

Syringa Lilac (see page 80).

Tamarix Tamarisk. Grow ***T. pentandra*** 'Pink Cascade' on clay. Feathery blue-green foliage and sprays of scented pink late summer flowers.

Pruning Cut down to 25 cm (10 in) above the ground in late winter or early spring.

Viburnum Stick to the following varieties on clay:

V. carlesii – deciduous spring flowering; ***V. opulus*** Guelder rose – deciduous summer flowering and autumn berries; ***V. tinus*** – evergreen, winter flowering and spring berrying.

Pruning Thin out weak and overcrowded shoots – evergeen leaves in spring, deciduous in autumn.

Problems Look out for whitefly and aphids.

Vinca Periwinkle. Green or variegated evergreens with

blue, mauve, purple or white spring flowers.

V. major – Greater periwinkle and ***V. m*** 'Variegata' are blue flowered and good on clay.

Pruning Clip to restrain in the summer months.

Weigela Stick to flowering hybrid varieties on clay – foxglove like flowers come in pinks, reds and white.

W. hybrida 'Abel Carriere', carmine; ***W. h.*** 'Bristol Ruby', wine-red; ***W. h.*** 'Eva Rathke', crimson-red; ***W. h.*** 'Mont Blanc', white.

Pruning Cut out overcrowded and the oldest flowered shoots after blooming.

Problems Aphid infestations.

Conifers
Chamaecyparis lawsoniana 'Allumii' (Cypress) and ***Taxus baccata*** (Common yew) are good hedging conifers for clay.

Pruning Clip in the spring and late summer.

Aquatics like orontium are excellent for the larger scale garden pool or bog garden. They make large spreading plants which quickly fill out.

HARDY PERENNIALS AND BEDDING PLANTS

Although hardy perennials embrace a whole range of varied plants, they are frequently catalogued according to their soil moisture needs or tolerances. This in turn leads to convenient groupings for special purposes – these have been adapted here.

Rock and alpine plants

In general, rock and alpine plants require to be planted in free-draining soil with their crowns resting slightly above the surrounding ground level to ensure adequate surface water run-off. Many of these plants are drought tolerant and resent wet roots during the winter months.

On clay soils, especially in areas of high rainfall, it is difficult, if not virtually impossible, to grow rock and alpine plants without completely changing the soil. In short, plants must be set out into pockets or beds of prepared compost. By adopting this practice, the tables are turned and almost any kind of rock or alpine plant can be grown given due regard to aspect and climate. When making your selections always be guided by your local garden centre.

Aquatic or pool plants

In the average modern garden pool, plants like waterlilies are grown in containers. They are also set out into prepared compost so there is no need to relate plant choice specifically to clay soil. Similarly with plants known as 'marginals' which are grown in shallow water. Here again containers are used and the choice is not confined to clay soil plants. In view of the fact that selections are made from the whole range of pool plants and marginals, these plants are not discussed further. Consult a good water garden catalogue for further details.

Clay-soil plants

As with trees and shrubs, the point should be made that waterlogged conditions will not be tolerated indefinitely, even with bog plants and other recognized moisture-loving perennials.

> **NOTE:** When planting perennials the crowns should always be set above the surrounding soil; with bog plants this means above the water level. This is necessary to provide adequate drainage and prevent root rot.

AT-A-GLANCE GUIDE – PLANTS FOR SPECIAL PURPOSES

Botanical name	Popular name	Uses
Acanthus	Bear's breeches	2 5
Aconitum	Monk's hood	2
Alchemilla	Lady's mantle	2 4 5 6
Anemone	Windflower	2 5 6

Annuals
Antirrhinum	Snapdragon	2 3 5 7
Callistephus	China aster	2 3 5 7
Impatiens	Busy lizzie	2 3 7
Lobelia	Lobelia, cardinal flower	2 3 7
Mimulus	Monkey flower	2 3 7
Tagetes	French marigold	2 3 7
Aruncus	Goat's beard	1 2 5 6
Astilbe	Spiraea	1 2 4 5 6 7
Astrantia	Masterwort	2 4 5
Bergenia	Bergenia	2 4 5 6
Brunnera	Giant forget-me-not	2 4 5 6

Bulbs
Camassia	Quamash	1 2 5 6
Crocosmia	Montbretia	2 5
Dierama	Wand flower	2 5
Narcissus	Daffodil	2 3 5 6 7
Caltha	Marsh marigold	1 2 4 5 6
Convallaria	Lily of the valley	2 4 5 6 7
Doronicum	Leopard's bane	2 4 5
Epimedium	Bishop's hat	2 4 6
Filipendula	Meadow sweet	1 2 4 5 6

Ferns
Asplenium	Hart's tongue fern	2 4 5 6 7
Athyrium	Lady fern	2 4 5 6
Dryopteris	Male fern	2 4 5 6
Matteuccia	Shuttlecock fern	2 4 5 6
Osmunda	Royal fern	1 2 4 5 6
Polypodium	Polypody fern	2 4 5 6 7

Grasses and sedges
Carex	Sedge	1 2 3 4 7
Eriophorum	Cotton grass	2 5 6

AT-A-GLANCE GUIDE

Key
1 = bog/waterside
2 = border or island bed
3 = bedding plant
4 = ground cover/under-planting
5 = cutting/floral arrangements
6 = naturalizing
7 = containers

Botanical name	Popular name	Uses
Luzula	Woodrush	2 4 6
Molinia	Moor grass	2 5 6
Phalaris	Gardener's garters	1 2 5 6
Gentiana	Gentian	2 4 5 6
Helleborus	Hellebore, Christmas rose	2 4 5 6
Hemerocallis	Day lily	1 2 4 5 6
Hosta	Plantain lily	1 2 4 5 6
Inula	Elecampane	2 5
Iris	Iris	1 2 6
Lamium	Dead nettle	2 4 7
Ligularia	Leopard plant	2
Lychnis	Campion	2 5
Lysimachia	Loosestrife	1 2 3 7
Lythrum	Purple loosestrife	1 2 5
Monarda	Bergamot	2 5
Myosotis	Forget-me-not	1 2 3 4 5 7
Paeonia	Paeony	2 5
Phlox	Border phlox	2 4 5 7
Polygonatum	Solomon's seal	2 4 5 6
Primula	Primula	1 2 3 4 5 6 7
Pulmonaria	Lungwort	2 5 6
Rheum	Rhubarb	2
Saxifraga	London pride	2 4 5
Solidago	Golden rod	2 4 5 7
Symphytum	Comfrey	2 4 5 6
Trollius	Globe flower	1 2 5 6

HARDY PERENNIALS AND BEDDING PLANTS FOR CLAY-DESCRIPTIVE GUIDE

S = propagate from seed
D = propagate from division

Acanthus Bear's breeches. Handsome leaves, tall rose, purple and white late summer flowers. (S, D).
Problems Not suitable for exposed gardens.

Aconitum Monk's hood. High spikes of hooded blue, white or pink flowers. (D)
Problems Poisonous flowers – but the likelihood of being eaten is rare. Needs shelter.

Alchemilla mollis – Lady's mantle – cloud-like sprays of tiny yellow flowers carried above soft green foliage. (D)

Anemone Windflowers. Stick to **A** x **hybrida** on clay. Different coloured late summer flowers. (D)

Annual summer bedding plants Use container-grown plants and set out with a good rootball of compost into well-prepared ground. See list on pages 93-4 for those most tolerant of clay.

Aruncus Goat's beard. Plumes of milky white summer flowers rise out of massed green leaves. (D)

Astilbe Bright summer flower plumes, ornamental, ferny green, bronze or bronze-purple foliage. (D)

Astrantia Masterwort. Unusual pink or whitish-green summer/autumn flowers.

Bergenia Bold glossy evergreen leaves, clusters of pink, crimson, purplish-pink or white spring flowers. (D)
Problems Don't expose to freezing winds and early morning sun.

Pontederia cordata *smothers weeds effectively at the margins of a pool. Best reserved for large spaces. Plant in plunged containers in a small garden.*

Brunnera Giant forget-me-not. This plant is a brilliant sky blue with spring and early summer flowers. (D)

Bulbs See list on page 93 for those best suited to clay. Don't plant any bulb deeper than two and a half times its diameter and set each bulb out on a handful of sand. The soil must be well prepared and free draining.
Problems In time most bulbs will rot on clay soils.

Caltha Marsh marigold. Yellow or ivory white-cupped spring flowers. (D)

Convallaria Lily of the valley. Arching spikes of lovely fragrant white late spring flowers. (D)

Doronicum Leopard's bane. Bright yellow early spring daisies. (D)

Epimedium Bishop's hat. Attractive semi-evergreen ground-cover foliage with pink, yellow or red spring flowers. (D)

Filipendula Meadowsweet. Frothy white or red summer flower heads, ferny foliage. They are useful for borders and are also excellent for water-side planting. (D)

Ferns See list on page 93 for a selection of ferns. Many others are also suitable.

Grasses, sedges and rushes. See pages 93-4 for a selection of those which can best be kept under control. Be wary of invasive kinds and those which will seed into neighbours' gardens – not always too popular! (D)

Gentiana asclepiada – Willow gentian. Blue, trumpet-shaped late summer flowers on arching stems.

Helleborus niger – Christmas rose. Glossy evergreen leaves and white winter flowers. (D)

Hemerocallis – Day lilies. Variously coloured, showy lily-like summer flowers. (D)

Hosta – Plantain lily. Bold, attractively coloured leaves; lily-like ivory, lilac or purple blue summer/autumn flowers. (D)

Inula royleana Large yellow daisy summer flowers. (D)

Iris Stick to *I. kaempferi; I. laevigata;* or *I. sibirica* on clay. All grown for their summer flowers. (D)

Lamium Dead nettles. Foliage plants with pink or white spring flowers. (D)
Problems Can be invasive.

Ligularia clivorum 'Desdemona' Leopard plant. Purplish leaves with long spikes of orange daisy-like summer flowers. (D)

Lychnis chalcedonica Maltese cross. Scarlet, rounded clusters of summer flowers. (D.S.)

Lysimachia Loosestrife. Beautiful summer flowering plants in yellow or white. (D)

Lythrum Purple loosestrife. Accent plants with pink, rose-red or crimson late summer flower spikes. (D)
Problems Not suitable for exposed gardens.

Monarda Bergamot. Colourful whorls of pink, red or purple summer/autumn flowers. (D)

Myosotis palustris 'Mermaid'. Water forget-me-not. Masses of tiny bright blue flowers from spring to mid-summer.

Paeonia officinalis varieties are the paeonies best suited to clay. They have majestic blooms and luxuriant foliage. (D)
Problems They will not flower when planted deep.

Phlox Different coloured large terminal summer/autumn flower clusters. (D)

Problems Subject to eelworm and mildew.

Polygonatum multiflorum Solomon's seal. Arching stems of greenish-white, bell-like spring flowers. (D)

Primula Select varieties of **P. denticulata; P. japonica; P. vulgaris.** All flower reliably on clay. (D)

Pulmonaria Lungwort. Bright spring flower sprays, some with foliage interest. (D)

Rheum Ornamental rhubarb. Large leaved accent plant with towering flower spikes. Choose a red variety. (D)

Saxifraga x **urbium** London pride. Dense mats with spires of tiny pink spring flowers. (D)

Solidago Golden rod. Late summer yellow mimosa-like flowers. (D)

Symphytum x **uplandicum** 'Variegatum' Comfrey. Startling white variegated leaves, drooping bell-shaped summer flowers. (D)

Trollius Globe flower. Large orange or yellow globular spring/summer flowers. (D)

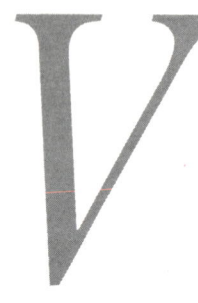

VEGETABLES AND FRUIT FOR CLAY SOILS

As with shrubs and flowers, many vegetables and fruits crop well on clay soils which have been looked after and thoroughly prepared. Some merely tolerate the conditions, but are still worth growing nonetheless. Others will not crop satisfactorily unless they are grown in raised beds or containers of prepared potting compost. This helps to overcome any limitations imposed by the original soil on site. In the main, attention is focussed in this chapter on popular varieties which crop well or at least give a worthwhile return on clay soils.

In general, on rich clay soils, there is a tendency for many crops to produce leaf at the expense of pods, roots and fruits. This may help to explain in part why leaf crops like cabbage grow so well. There also tends to be more of a physical barrier to root growth and movement than on sandy loams. Some root crops, in fact, have great difficulty in adapting to clay soils.

Foliage shrubs provide colour in partially shaded borders. They are useful for infilling vertical as well as horizontal spaces. Many require minimal attention.

The importance of variety

Not only is it necessary to select crops best suited to clay soils, but also to choose the right variety. With apples, for instance, cooking varieties tend to be easier to grow than dessert. Also, because clay soils warm up very slowly in the spring, it is usually better to concentrate on growing mid-season crops rather than early. With root crops like beetroot, carrots and parsnips, the shallow rooted, round or stumpy varieties are more likely to be successful than the deep rooting long types. They score on two counts: first less energy is used up penetrating the heavy soil; and secondly most shorter rooting varieties are quicker maturing.

Cultivations and management

Due allowance must always be made for climate and soil conditions, including crop rotation and pest and disease control. The importance of thorough soil preparation, adequate drainage, generous manuring, liming where necessary plus timely operations and attention to detail cannot be overstressed.

Nowhere is the practice of sowing seeds indoors and planting out into containers more valuable than on clay soils. The object is to transplant sturdy young plants into their cropping positions with a good, established rootball. This overcomes many problems with crops like cauliflowers, cabbages and beans. In the case of shallots, bulbing onions and garlic, start the sets or segments off in pots in early spring giving them a temperature of 7°C (45°F). Harden off gradually in mid to late spring and plant out into cropping positions.

Fig. 9. Grow potatoes on ridges to improve drainage and encourage the soil to warm up quickly.

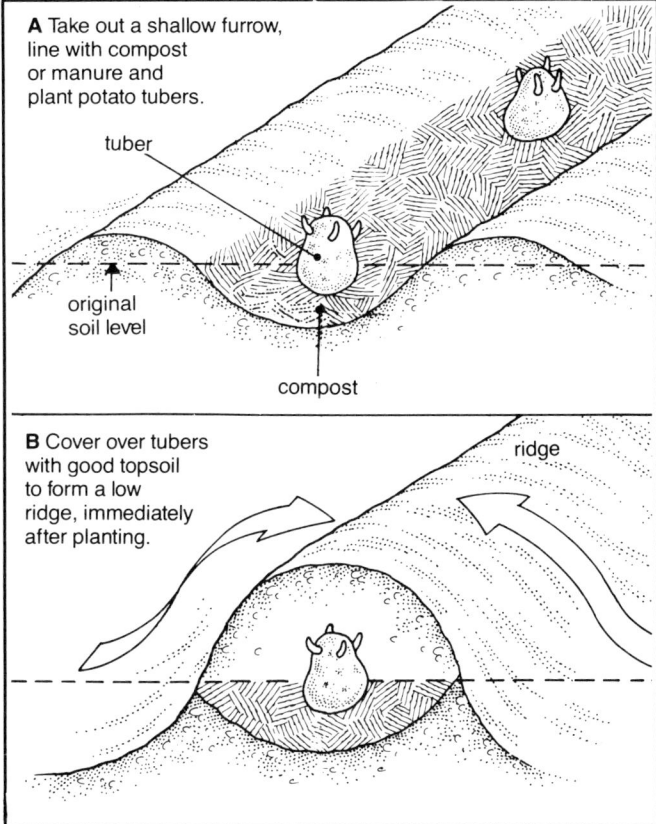

A Take out a shallow furrow, line with compost or manure and plant potato tubers.

tuber

original soil level

compost

B Cover over tubers with good topsoil to form a low ridge, immediately after planting.

ridge

In general allow more generous inter-row spacings to accommodate the greater anticipated top growth. And when drawing up ridges for potatoes, turnips and swedes make them up to a quarter as far apart again as you would normally. Ridges can then be kept earthed up more easily, to get rid of excess moisture.

The value of cloches

Cloches are a particularly good investment for a vegetable garden on clay soil. They are of enormous value early and late in the season. In spring they are excellent for warming up and drying out the soil prior to sowing seed or setting out indoor raised plants like beans and salads. They also give good protection to the germinating seeds and young plants until they become well established. By this time the more tender tomatoes, cucumbers, sweet corn and marrows will be ready for setting outdoors, and again will most certainly benefit from some cover for a little while until they are growing steadily. In autumn use cloches to protect any late maturing salads and similar vegetables, or to cover ripening onions, shallots and tomatoes.

Key
* = Ideal clay soil plants
T = Transplanted container-raised plants
SS = Sown in situ
Pl = Set out tubers, sets or roots

VEGETABLES

Crop		Where and how to grow in clay soil garden	Position
*Beans, broad	T	Prepared ground	sun
Beans, dwarf	T	Container, raised bed, prepared trenches	sun
Beans, runner	T	Container, prepared trench	sun
Beetroot (round vars)	SS	Prepared drills, raised bed, container	sun or semi-shade
*Brussel sprouts (mid-season vars)	T	Prepared ground	sun
*Cabbage	T	Prepared ground	sun or semi-shade
Carrot (round & stumpy vars)	SS	Prepared drills, raised bed, container	sun
Cauliflower (autumn & spring heading vars)	T	Prepared ground	sun

Crop		Where and how to grow in clay soil garden	Position
Celery (self-blanching vars)	T	Prepared ground	sun
Chicory	T	Prepared ground	sun or
	SS	Prepared drills	semi-shade
Cucumber	T	Raised bed or container	sun
Garlic	PL	Prepared ground, raised bed	sun
*Kale (curly leaved vars)	T	Prepared ground	sun or semi-shade
*Kohl rabi	SS	Prepared drills	sun
*Leek (long trench vars)	T	Prepared ground	sun
Lettuce	T	Prepared ground, raised bed, container	sun or semi-shade
Marrow/ courgette	T	Raised bed, container	sun
Melon	T	Raised bed, container with frame protection	sun
Onion, salad	SS	Prepared drills, raised bed, container	sun
Onion, bulbing	T Pl	Prepared ground, raised bed, container	sun
Parsnip (short rooted quick maturing vars)	SS	Prepared drills	sun or semi-shade
Pea (dwarf early vars)	SS	Prepared trenches .	sun
Potato	Pl	Prepared trenches, container	sun
Pumpkin & squash	T	Raised bed, container	sun
Radish	SS	Prepared drills, raised bed, container	sun
*Rhubarb	Pl	Prepared ground	sun or semi-shade
Shallot	Pl	Prepared ground, raised bed, container	sun
Spinach (summer vars)	SS	Prepared drills	sun or semi-shade

Crop	Where and how to grow in clay soil garden		Position
Spinach (perpetual)	SS	Prepared drills	sun or semi-shade
*Sprouting broccoli	T	Prepared ground	sun
Swede	SS	Prepared drills	sun
Sweetcorn	T	Prepared ground, raised bed	sun
Tomato	T	Prepared ground, raised bed	sun
Turnip	SS	Prepared drills	sun

POPULAR HERBS

*Chives	Pl T	Prepared ground, raised bed	sun
Marjoram	T	Container, raised bed	sun
*Mint	Pl	Prepared ground	sun or semi-shade
Parsley	T	Prepared ground, raised bed, container	sun or semi-shade
Sage	Pl T	Prepared ground, raised bed, container	sun
Thyme	Pl	Container, raised bed	sun

Berberis, plum, cherry and forsythia are suitable hardy shrubs and trees for heavy, well-drained soils. Try forsythia as a colourful hedge.

POPULAR FRUITS

Crop	Where and how to grow in clay soil garden			
	Prepared Ground	Container	Raised-bed Planting box	Position
Apple (culinary vars on dwarf rootstocks)	+	+	−	sun
Blackberry	+	−	−	sun
Cherry (Morello)	+	+	+	sun and semi-shade
Currant – black	+	−	−	sun and semi-shade
Currant – red and white	+	+	+	sun, give shelter
Gooseberry (culinary vars)	+	+	+	sun and semi-shade
Grape	−	+	+	sun and shelter
Loganberry	+	−	−	sun
Nectarine (early vars)	−	+	+	sun and shelter
Peach (early vars)	−	+	+	sun and shelter
Pear (culinary vars on dwarf rootstocks)	+	+	+	sun
Plum/gage (dual purpose & culinary vars on dwarf rootstocks)	+	−	−	sun
Raspberry (summer fruiting vars)	+	−	−	sun and semi-shade
Strawberry (summer fruiting vars)	+	+	+	sun and semi-shade

ANAGEMENT AND AFTERCARE

Preparation and planting are only a part, albeit an important part, of gardening. Aftercare is just as vital if the time and money expended on setting out good plants on well prepared land is to pay fruitful dividends.

Be ever mindful, throughout the following pages, of the need to consider the overall effect of all aspects of cultivations interlinked one with another, rather than considering each in total isolation.

SHELTER AND PROTECTION

Wind

Newly set out plants and seedlings are particularly vulnerable to the ill effects of high winds, but on clay soils wind damage is by no means limited to just the young or the newly planted: established plantings are also liable to injury. Drying out, scorching and mechanical damage are normally associated with strong winds, but trees and shrubs on clay are particularly liable to suffer from 'windrock'. Basically, the movement of stems at soil level creates a cavity in which water lodges and subsequent rotting soon sets in. Windrock is more of a problem on rich clay soils largely because plants tend to make growth vigorous, and present a larger surface area to catch the wind.

A combination of preventive measures is advisable to minimize windrock. Shelter screening, firm staking and tying of plants, earthing up or soiling over around the plants are all good measures to implement. And, in some cases, pruning to reduce plant size is a good idea. Plant choice, as mentioned earlier, is also important. For instance, when planting in coastal districts on high ground or in any exposed inland garden, choose low ground cover. Alternatively choose varieties which allow the wind to filter through rather than create too solid a barrier – the flowering plum and tamarisk are useful candidates for this purpose. Also select wind-firm varieties like rowan, whitebeam, forsythia and flowering currant, which are noted for their strong rootholds.

Permanent wind screens
These come in various guises.

Aim to buy one with about 50% permeability; it will cause less air turbulance than a solid wall or fence (see page 21). The screen height across the direction of oncoming wind is an important factor too. Expect a long, straight screen to shelter a level strip on the leeward side equal to at least seven times the screen height (see page 56).

Temporary screens These are useful for individual plants or small groups and are easily made using fine mesh netting fixed to a supporting frame. They are invaluable with new plants until they are established firmly. Screen on three sides and wherever possible back the screens into the direction of the prevailing winds.

Nurse plants Consider the use of temporary quick growing filler plants or strategically placed nurse plants to shield slower growing long term choice plants. They are often worthwhile, provided they are removed before they cause any overcrowding.

Rain, hail and snow

Only limited help is practical. Cover young plants at risk from these conditions with cloches or some fine mesh netting. In cold districts, after heavy falls of snow, it is advisable to gently knock the snow off evergreens and conifers, if you feel there is any likelihood of the plants being forced out of shape. Pruning (see page 116) can also be of help in this respect by reducing crown size. With most low growing plants it is best to leave snow cover undisturbed since it helps to give added protection against icy winds and frost.

Sun

Very young plants and those recently set out are vulnerable to too much strong sun. Frozen leaves and buds are likely to be damaged too in late winter and spring. Most at risk, however, are the evergreens and spring flowering plants which are exposed to early morning sun after an overnight frost. In all cases covering with fine mesh netting to shade can help.

Frost

Careful timing for planting out tender plants in spring is necessary. Wait until all danger of frost has passed, if plants are not to suffer a setback. Also be careful lifting all marginally tender and frost-sensitive plants in autumn. They should be moved indoors to overwinter, before the first autumn frosts.

SUPPORTING AND TYING

As previously discussed, the need for adequate supports and tying is usually more necessary on clay soils than with other soils – as you tend to get more lush growth and larger plants.

The first point to be made is that supports in general need to be stronger than on most other soils otherwise there is a risk of significant harmful movement. Tree stakes also need to be longer, to allow them to be sunk deeper. A minimum 60-75 cm (2-2½ ft) below ground with 1.2-1.8 m (4-6 ft) above ground is about right. Use the same ratio for longer or shorter supports. The normal method of staking free-standing standard trees is to use a single stake with at least two ties, one fixed near the top and the other half way down (see page 68). When staking full standards with a minimum 1.8 m (6 ft) clear stem, it is worth the extra trouble and expense of providing double stakes with cross bars for added support. Double staking is recommended too with trees like thorn, laburnum and crab apple. These trees tend to quickly make largish crowns, but are without a firm roothold in the early years of growth, result-

Hypericum is a reliable shrub for sun or partial shade. Use it with herbaceous plants as here, or as underplanting beneath trees where height allows.

ing in a leaning tree. This is a problem often faced by clay soil gardeners: they have an established but leaning tree! If the tree is not too large, prevent it from leaning any further by driving in a stake at a 45° angle – rather like a prop. The trunk is tied to the top of the stake.

Since stakes are needed for a few years more than normal on other soils, always use treated larch or hardwood timber.

Wall plants and climbers also need stronger, secure supports to take account of the weight of extra growth. Here wall-mounted trellis panels have much to recom-

mend them. Always aim to leave a 3-4 cm (1-1½ in) gap between the trellis and wall. Not only does this reduce the risk of plants like ivy from damaging the masonry, but also makes it easier to tie in plants while ensuring a more even distribution of weight.

When training plants up wall supports, leave sufficient slack on the stem to allow for movement and settlement of the soil because of wet weather, drying and freezing. Differences of 15-20 cm (6-8 in) are quite commonplace over a 12 month period. One useful point to remember here is to set the trellis no closer to the ground than about 40 cm (16

The double flowered Kerria japonica 'Pleniflora' is the best variety for clay – as here. This shrub has distinctive winter green stems and yellow spring flowers.

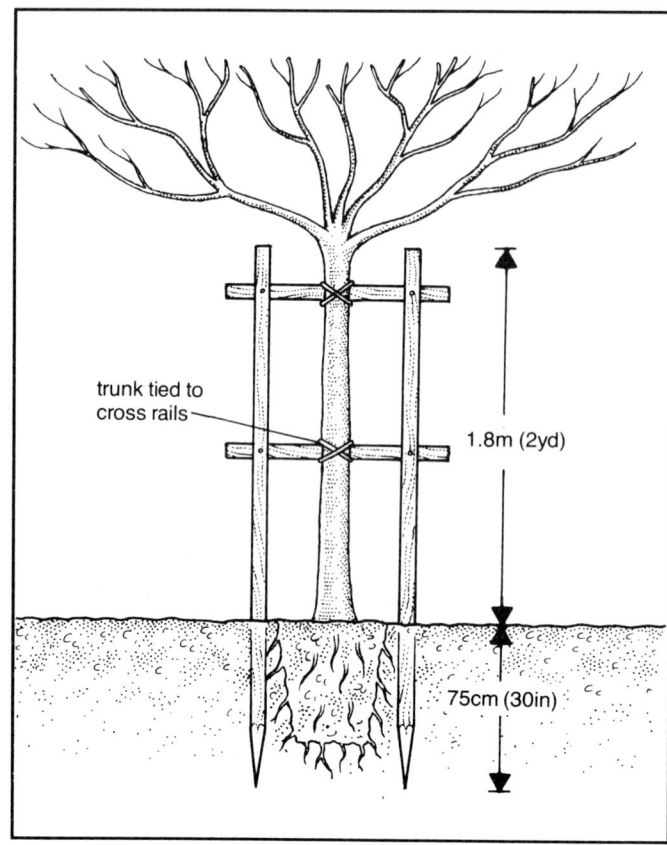

circle of canes and strings or proprietary hoops for tall clump formers like monarda, lychnis and heleniums; and twiggy pieces of stick pushed among the stems of shorter plants like dwarf golden rod.

Among the vegetables, Brussels sprouts and tall sprouting broccoli need cane supports to reduce windrock. Crops like peas and beans should be supported in the normal way over pea or bean sticks or on netting.

FEEDING

Although the general principles of plant nutrition are much the same, there are a few special points to watch out for on clay soils.

The nutrients

Because of the very nature of the soil less nitrogen is required, but the potassium levels need boosting. This will help to correct any tendency to lush growth. In practice, most plants will thrive on balanced high-potash tomato type feeds. Since every effort should be made to encourage good root formation and early maturity when gardening on clay, make sure there is no shortage of phosphate either. Phosphates promote early maturity and healthy root growth.

Fig. 10. Double staking is recommended for trees which quickly form large crowns – before their roots become windfirm.

in). Train the plant along tarred twine attached at one end to a peg near the plant, and at the other end to the bottom of the trellis.

Many herbaceous perennials and annuals like tall antirrhinums and kochsia, which are self supporting on sandy loams, need to be staked on clays. The more usual methods of support include: individual canes for stems of tall spiked varieties like delphiniums; a triangle or

Trace nutrients

Because clay soils are naturally richer in plant nutrients, there is less likelihood of trace nutrient deficiency on these soils.

Alkaline fertilizers

It is best to avoid using alkaline fertilizers like nitrate of soda which contain considerable amounts of sodium. These fertilizers only tend to make clay soils even more sticky and difficult to work.

Dry top dressings versus liquid feeding

Dry top dressings come into their own on clay soils and can be very labour saving. Since nutrients and moisture are retained for longer periods dry feeds are longer lasting and fewer applications are needed. However, it must be said that liquid and foliar feeds are just as important on clay soils as on any other, where a rapid response is needed to correct mineral deficiencies such as iron or magnesium. They are just as important when growing plants in containers.

Timing

When feeding any plants on clay soils, applications are best confined to spring and early summer. Feeding late in the year on clay is more likely to result in soft, lush growth, liable to frost and winter injury, more than on other soils. This is of particular significance when it comes to lawns, fruits and winter vegetables.

With fruit trees and bushes it is usual to top dress annually in late winter or early spring, using a complete, balanced fertilizer. In view of the short growing season this ensures that they do not suffer any nutrient deficiency.

WATERING

As discussed previously clay soils are notorious for retaining moisture. But during prolonged hot weather, even these soils dry out, and irrigation will become necessary. The need to start watering before the soil dries out cannot be emphasized too strongly when dealing with clay soils. If left too late, the soil becomes dry and hard baked and is extremely difficult to get moist again. In fact, watering on clay soils is never easy. This is mainly because water penetration is slow at the best of times. And if water is given to the soil too quickly, surface water run off and soil erosion very often result. Slow and timely watering is the key to success.

Lawns

Proceed in careful stages

when dealing with cracked and dried out lawns. This often occurs when they have been grassed down without a rubble raft and without prepared topsoil (see page 32). First damp over the surface using a watering can fitted with a fine rose and filled with water plus a dash of washing-up liquid. This should largely overcome the difficulties of 'wetting' the surface. Next slowly apply sufficient water to moisten the top 6 mm (¼ in) of soil, preferably using a fine sprinkler or a can with a fine rose. Always check that there is no ban on watering before you start! The following day the lawn should be ready to lightly spike. Use a garden fork and work systematically over the whole area, going down vertically to 8 cm (3 in) or more if possible, at about 20 cm (8 in) intervals. Then turn on the sprinkler again slowly, aiming to apply 1 cm (½ in) of water over a period of 48 hours. This is the equivalent of 10 l per sq m (2 gal per sq yd) if using a can.

Plants

Generally speaking, individual plants are usually best watered by drenching the rootball thoroughly, rather than wetting the entire area.

With *newly planted* shrubs, and largish plants, sink a plant pot up to the rim near the roots. Make sure it has drainage holes in the base and line with a plastic bag perforated with pin prick sized holes. Thereafter keep the pot filled with water during dry weather and this will ensure that water always gets down to the roots.

Where there are numerous *young plants,* as with bedding or vegetables, it is often easier to blanket the whole area with moisture. But first loosen up the soil's surface crust. Apply the water slowly, in a mist from a sprinkler or fine rose droplets from a can. Heavy droplets can lead to surface crusting and compaction. When watering *rows of plants* you will find that the seep or weep hose works particularly well, provided it is used correctly.

When watering *prior to mulching or topdressing* with fertilizers, always loosen the soil crust first, and then thoroughly spike with a fork where the soil has started to dry out to loosen it yet further.

NOTE: Never use water from a domestic water softener for irrigation, especially if it uses sodium-based salts. You will risk sticky soil and sick plants if you do.

Flowering currant is a good plant for any garden. Use it for hedging, as a specimen shrub or as a wall plant. It stands clipping to restrain.

SOIL MANAGEMENT

This involves maintaining and improving the condition and fertility of the soil.

Lawncare

The main aims here are to relieve compaction, improve soil aeration and assist the drainage. Where lawns have been properly laid (see page 32) serious problems should not arise for many years ahead. It is the lawns which were hastily laid on inadequately prepared soil which spell future disaster, and call for urgent remedial measures.

Spiking of the soil is needed whenever and wherever water lies on the soil's surface for any length of time after prolonged, steady rain. Working from planks, spike the ground with a fork at 15 cm (6 in) intervals. Follow this by top dressing the soil with some sand brushed well into the holes to help keep them open. A more effective treatment, which is slower and much heavier work, is hollow tine forking. It is carried out in much the same way as spiking, but uses a hollow tine fork instead of an ordinary garden fork. Small cores or plugs of soil are removed and bigger holes left. Subsequent top dressing with potting compost, brushed well into the holes, is the standard procedure to follow. This work is best completed in the early autumn.

The rolling of a lawn must not be overdone. It should only be carried out if the lawn is puffy after winter frosts or following the regular use of a hover mower. Roll lightly, so that it is just sufficient to firm up the surface and ensure a good level for subsequent mowing. In spring, it is definitely best to wait until the ground has dried out completely before rolling again.

BEDS AND BORDERS

Beds and borders in spring

As soon as the soil surface has dried out sufficiently for you to work on it, gently refirm the soil around the roots of any young plants loosened by strong winds or frost. Cover any exposed roots with potting compost or planting mix, and fill in any collar cavities at the base of plants which have suffered from windrock. If the effects of windrock are very pronounced, and the soil has formed a hard – possibly wet and shiny – collar, more drastic measures are called for. Before top dressing with potting compost, carefully break up the collar.

Having given priority to the

firming and top dressing of exposed roots, loosen and break up the surface crust around the remainder of the bed and border by going over the surface lightly with a fork and removing weeds at the same time. Take great care not to go down too deeply nor to loosen or dislodge any garden plants. If the soil is inclined to be sticky, take the opportunity to work sand, peat or other organic matter into the soil to improve the texture. After loosening the surface crust top dress with some fertilizer where appropriate (see page 109).

Spring is a good time to mulch using well rotted garden compost, manure, peat or even bark in some form (see page 38). Once the soil has warmed up and is still moist and weedfree, aim to spread a minimum 5-8 cm (2-3 in) layer of mulch. This acts as a good smother for weed seedlings, slows down the surface evaporation and prevents surface crusting. Never be tempted to apply mulches too early in the year as they will act as insulators and will slow down the natural seasonal warming up process of the soil. Also if snow and ice are inadvertently buried, the thawing out process is delayed. Most trees, shrubs, climbers, perennials, and bush, cane and tree fruits should be mulched in early to mid spring – always be guided by climate and season.

Beds and borders in summer

Where beds and borders are mulched generously in spring, little else is needed by way of cultivation during the summer months, apart from some hand weeding and replenishing of the mulches.

In the absence of mulching, regular loosening and stirring of the soil crust, plus regular weeding, becomes essential. Because clay soils pack down hard, it is more difficult to break up the surface crust than on light loams where hoeing is usually done with a swoe or Dutch hoe. Where the improvement of the texture of clay soil still has a long way to go, it is usual to loosen the soil crust by going over it lightly with a garden fork. Alternatively pulling a triple tined cultivator through the soil with a chopping action can be very effective.

Another chopping tool which finds favour on heavy soils is the draw hoe. It is an invaluable tool since it is also used for earthing up. The Chillington hoe and Chillington fork are worth seeking out too. Old gardeners will remember the Chillington hoe as an undisguised Canterbury

Opposite:
Herbaceous plants in subtle blends of lime green, white and lavender. The effect is strengthened with a touch of red from the lilies.

Below: *A mix of moisture loving herbaceous plants provide colour and interest from spring to autumn. Many are suitable for difficult, partly shaded spots.*

hoe, much used on the clay soils of Kent up to the 1940s. Regular loosening of the soil crust is an advisable task throughout the summer. It kills weeds, allows plant roots to breathe, assists rain and irrigation water to penetrate, and is a necessary preliminary to earthing up. Crops like potatoes and Brussels sprouts are earthed up during the summer.

One useful and effective way to improve clay soils is to scatter and rake in some gypsum during the late spring or summer while the surface is loose. If you give a very thorough raking in, gypsum applied at the rate 200 g per sq m (6 oz per sq yd), will form water stable granules and generally improve the soil's texture considerably.

Beds and borders in autumn and winter

It is sound practice to earth up young trees and shrubs sometime during early to mid-autumn. This is especially important in exposed gardens as an aid against windrock. Don't mound the soil up more than 5-8 cm (2-3 in) against the stems or trunks. Similarly, remember to earth up vegetables like sprouts, cabbage and broccoli which are to stand during the winter months.

Autumn is also a good time to fork over the spaces between plants in beds and borders, removing weeds and debris and working in a dressing of coarse sand, plus the remains of summer mulches of compost, manure, peat and pulverised or composted bark. Don't disturb any bark chips and gravel. A narrow border fork is a useful implement for working between plants in confined spaces. When forking in the autumn don't break down the lumps too finely, it is better to leave a rough surface to cope with the weathering action of rain, frost and wind. If the soil is very weedy with large numbers of seedlings, like chickweed, in evidence skim them off before forking. Alterna-tively, if the seedling weeds are very small, and space allows, bury them completely by shallow digging down to about 15 cm (6 in), taking care not to damage the plant roots.

Where beds and borders missed spring mulching, try to work in a generous dressing of manure or compost to improve soil in the autumn.

Some three to four weeks after forking or digging the beds and borders, lime the soil as necessary. About a handful per sq m (1 sq yd) of ground limestone makes an average dressing (see page 45).

Bog garden and waterside

Clean up around plants in the spring and mulch with peat or leafmould during mid- to late spring. Keep the area weed-free in summer, and it is sound practice to earth up and deepen the hollows between plants during the autumn. This helps to drain winter rains away from the crowns of plants.

Rock and alpine plants

Provided that they are planted in pockets of prepared soil mix, and the drainage is reasonable, the treatment of rock and alpine plants is the same as for any average garden soil. Keep weedfree, and top dress in the spring and

Fig. 11. Summer prune to contain vigour and ripen growth wood.

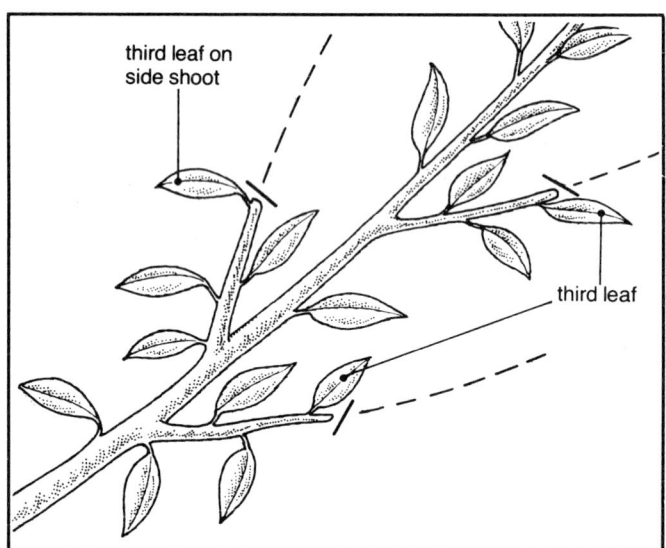

third leaf on side shoot

third leaf

autumn using potting compost topped with gravel.

PRUNING, TRAINING AND KEEPING TIDY

At first glance there might seem to be little difference between the treatment on clay soils and on average loams. However, in practice, even quite a small variation in timing or technique often tips the scales in favour of success or failure.

On clay soils there is usually a strong tendency for many trees, shrubs, perennials, fruits and vegetables to grow excessively. And all too often this means leaf and stem production at the expense of flowers, fruits and roots. Another major problem, especially in cold climate areas, is for plants to have too short a growing season. This is largely because plants on clay soils start slowly each spring, normally some three to four weeks later than those on light soils in the same area. The effect is a relatively short growing season before the autumn frosts set in. The result is two-fold: firstly, delayed flowering or harvesting of seeds, fruits and root crops: secondly, poor ripening of growth wood with a consequential risk of damaging winter injury.

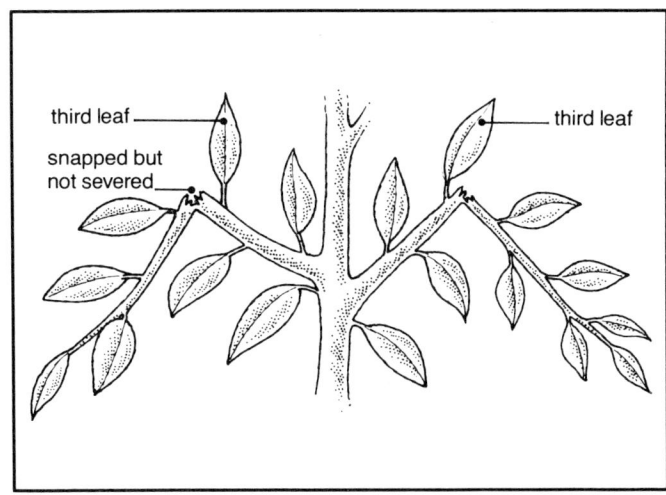

Fig. 12. Pruning diverts excess energy into flower and bud development.

Pruning

This helps in various ways, particularly when used in conjunction with training. Generally speaking, summer pruning reduces vigorous plant growth and lets in light and air to ripen both fruits and growth wood. Autumn and early winter pruning tend to result in increased growth and diminished crops especially if there has been hard cut back. Light pruning at this time encourages less new growth, but more early flowers. The same broad comments apply to rose pruning in the spring.

Fruits like apples and pears, gooseberries, red and white currants, benefit from shortening the side shoots back to three leaves during the summer. It is also good practice to tip new shoots of

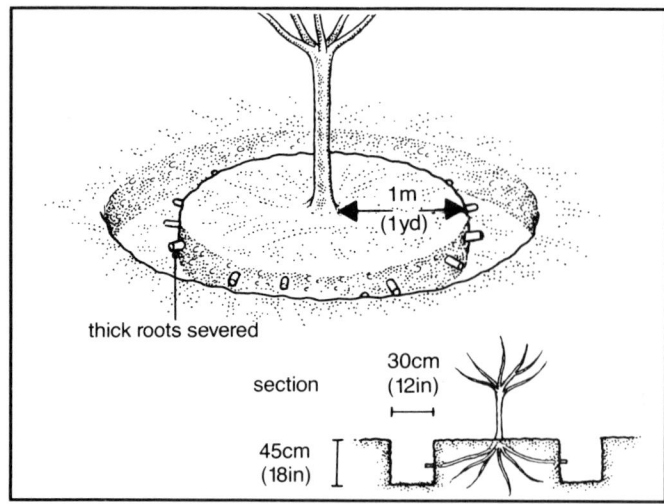

thick roots severed

section

30cm (12in)

45cm (18in)

Above: Fig. 13. An extreme measure where stone fruits put on excess growth at the expense of fruiting.

ciduous hedging plants are best clipped in late summer instead of leaving until winter as is usual on average soils.

Autumn tipping back of new growths by one quarter to a third on bush roses and various other summer and autumn flowering shrubs, will effectively help to reduce windrock.

The practice of brutting apple, pear and flowering quinces, to promote flower and bud development and mop up excess energy, is a well known, and acceptable and effective technique used on the continent. In mid to late summer, the new season's shoots are bent downwards until they snap. The tips are left to hang down still attached until early autumn

cane fruits like blackberry and loganberry.

Strong growing shrubs like forsythia, flowering currant and flowering quince, benefit from pruning or clipping back new growth in late summer. And similarly many de-

Right: Fig. 14. Horizontally trained branches are more likely to produce flowers and fruits along their full length, when compared to those growing vertically.

espalier apple   climbing rose

Monarda – variety 'Cambridge Scarlet' can be relied on to provide a bold splash of colour on wet soils. They look well when contrasted with foliage plants or flowers.

Below: Fig. 15.   Young shoots are arched over and pegged down – a method of horizontal training suited to apple and plum.

when they are cut off. After brutting, the buds just below the snap plump up and form new flower buds.

If stone fruits like plum, greengage and damson grow excessively at the expense of fruiting, they are best pruned at the roots. This is instead of top pruning which is liable to result in canker and dieback. Root pruning would be carried out once or at the most twice during the life of a tree. Excavate a 30 cm (12 in) wide trench about 45 cm (18 in)

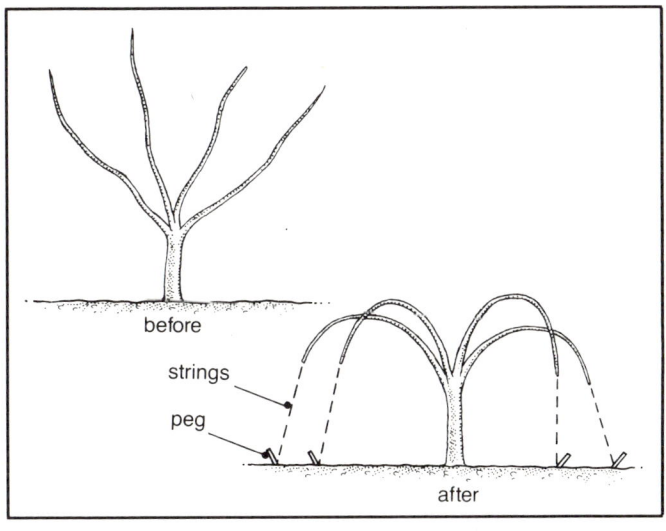

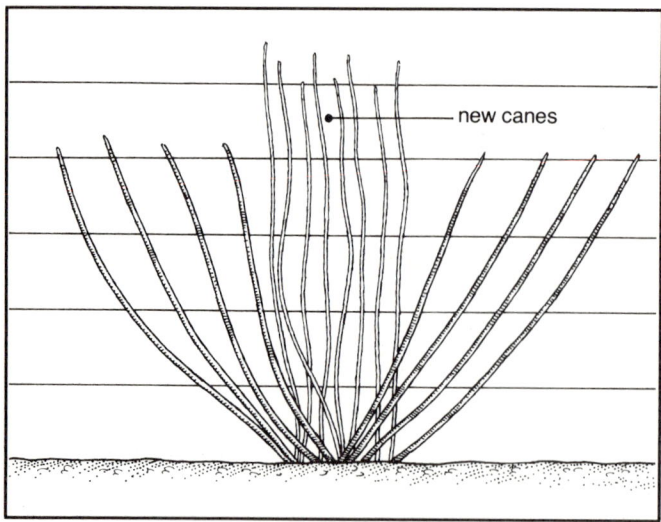

new canes

Fig. 16.   Grow blackberries as fans to restrain vigorous growth and encourage earlier ripening by letting in light and air.

deep and 1 m (3¼ ft) out from the trunk. Cut through all the thick roots crossing the trench, but disturb the fibrous ones as little as possible. Systematically replace the top soil, gently firming as the filling proceeds and working in some extra peat and sand.

Stopping, stripping and disbudding

Various plants, including chrysanthemums, dahlias and tall herbaceous perennials like michaelmas daisies, if stopped in early summer will often flower more prolifically on shorter plants. To ensure earlier flowering and better quality blooms, restrict the number of flower shoots to three or four per plant. Disbud plants like chrysanthemums, dahlias and large-

flowered roses, leaving the terminal or main leader bud to grow, all the secondary buds alongside and below are removed.

Training

It is not always realized that the manner in which trees and shrubs are trained has an important bearing on future flowering and fruiting. Stems and branches which grow or are trained horizontally, or dip slightly below the horizontal, are much more likely to produce flowers and fruits along their full length when compared to vertical growing plants. Advantage can be taken of this fact with fruit trees like apples and pears, and with climbing roses. Train all their branches out horizontally; espalier apples and pears provide good examples of such treatment.

Festooning is a relatively recent form of training, which is based on the above principle. It works well with apple and plum trees. New shoots are allowed to grow normally in their first season, then in autumn shoots are arched over and the tips trained earthwards and tied down.

PEST AND DISEASE CONTROL

Each soil type tends to develop certain plant ailments and infestation from pests.

Slugs and snails
These pests inevitably rank highly among the problems associated with clay soils. Clean cultivation work, elimination of weeds, removal of litter and clean hedge bottoms, plus regular year round baiting goes a long way towards keeping these difficult pests in check.

Root rots and wilts
Fungal, bacterial and virus attacks, are familiar features on clay soils. They take a hold if plants have been weakened by unfavourable soil conditions or neglect. Keep under control by practising crop rotation, improving the soil texture and drainage removing any diseased plants and a good rootball of soil promptly, and then disinfecting before replanting. When planting bulbs set them on a bed of sand (see page 96).

Chrysanthemum eelworm
This pest attacks many crops from tomatoes to ferns and herbaceous perennials and is encouraged by the moist conditions common to clay soils. Stunted weakly plants together with signs of wilting and drying off of lower leaves are typical danger signs. Af-

ter an attack you will need to destroy infected plants without delay. Replace them with woody plants like shrubs, and limit the growing of herbaceous perennials and annuals to containers of fresh compost for a minimum of four or five years. In the interim period set about improving the soil texture and drainage.

Disorders
Non-infectious diseases or disorders due to unfavourable growing conditions must not be underestimated in clay soils. They are probably among some of the most likely problems which will be encountered. Typical problems are:

Bud dropping on sweet peas and runner beans planted out too early in cold soils.

Premature fruit dropping of dessert apples, pears and cherries can be expected where the soil is cold and drainage is poor. The remedies have been discussed in previous chapters (see page 29-36).

Chilling The blueing of leaves and stems of plants set out in cold clay soils is a problem which causes severe setback and is very often en-

countered when growing tomatoes. Avoid chilling by growing plants in a sheltered spot in containers and delaying planting out until the soil temperature has reached 13° C (55° F).

Fanging and forking Root crops such as carrots and parsnips often develop deformed, forked roots. This is a problem which can arise on any stony soil, or any soil which has been freshly manured, and on clay soils which are over compacted. Grow short rooted varieties, preferably in raised beds.

Reverting On clay soils many variegated trees, shrubs and climbers make heavy growth and produce reverted green leaved shoots at a greater rate than usual. The reverted shoots grow more rapidly than the variegated. They will need to be cut out promptly.

Delayed flowering and ripening An abundance of moisture and a plentiful supply of nitrogen in the soil can appreciably delay flowering and the ripening of fruit. This is a problem which is also aggravated by shade. Use a high potash tomato-type fertilizer and prune and train the plants to overcome excess growth (as mentioned under pruning and training), and then take steps to let in the light and some sun.

Blackberries grow well in moist, heavy soils but tend to make excessive growth and need to be restrained.

Trollius makes a good splash of colour in sun or shade on clay soil.

APPENDIX

WHERE TO SEE CLAY GARDENS

If you are looking for design and planting ideas, it is a fairly natural reaction to want to go and see examples of established gardens on clay. Unfortunately, there are very few true clay soil gardens around today. This is because untreated, clay soil is very difficult to manage, much more so than the average sandy soil. While many large gardens, both public and private, have been successfully created on what was originally clay soil, caution is urged when visiting. Things are not quite what they at first appear. For when visiting any garden never take it for granted that the soil type and depth is uniform, and do bear in mind that clay soils can be acid, neutral or alkaline – each with it's own individual flora.

Frequently the soil in beds and planting areas has been altered out of all recognition. Very often in public parks – and in some of the older, well-known private gardens – the original clay soil was dug out and replaced with good topsoil. Just for the record, much of the more recent work of resoiling beds and borders

was carried out during the great depression earlier this century – as was the creation of artificial lakes, ponds and mounds – to give employment to otherwise unemployed labourers. In other gardens there is evidence that vast quantities of manure and sand – together with generous lime applications – have been used to alter the physical character of the soil. While it is acknowledged that clay burning to lighten the soil was much practiced, it is rarely undertaken these days.

Visits organized through a local garden club, and to members with clay soil gardens, can prove most helpful. Even if for no other reason the so called ecological approach of choosing plants to suit the local site and soil is more likely to be seen in small gardens – as an alternative to changing or altering the soil. National Trust gardens and those under the National Gardens scheme are usually well worth visiting. Check on the main season of interest beforehand. Don't ignore botanic gardens or local parks and public gardens – many often have much to offer. Note particularly those gardens which are highly reputed for their roses, bog and waterside planting – they probably have areas of clay. Useful sources of information on local gardens open to the public include libraries, garden societies, the local press, and the yellow pages of the telephone directory for the relevant areas.

Alton Towers, North of Uttoxeter, Staffs
5 miles N of Uttoxeter off the B5032. Ponds, fountains and gardens on the grand scale.

Breccles Hall, Norfolk
Stream and water garden.

Buscot Park, Faringdon, Berks
Mid-way between Faringdon and Lechlade on the A417. Lake and canal gardens – with formal gardens.

Cambridge University Botanic Gardens, Cambridge
Entrances off the A10, A604, Bateman Street and Brooklands Avenue. An interesting botanic garden.

Chartwell, Westerham, Kent
2 miles S of Westerham off the B2026. Rose gardens and water features.

Easton Neston, Towcester, Northants
Formal garden with ponds.

East Lambrook Manor, South of Martock, Somerset
4 miles NE of Ilminster on the road from Pluckington (B3168) to Stapleton (B3165). A noted small clay garden.

Sezincote, Gloucestershire
SW of Moreton-in-Marsh. Intereting water garden, trees and plants.

Tatton Park, Cheshire
N of Knutsford. Large ornamental gardens, formal and informal with waterside plantings.

Thorne's Park, Wakefield, Yorks
Large rose garden.

Savill Gardens, Berks
1½ miles from Egham in Wick Lane, Englefield Green, approximately 1 mile W of the A30. Waterside planting, exotic trees and shrubs.

BIBLIOGRAPHY
Current catalogues:
Blooms of Bressingham, Diss, Norfolk
Hillier's Nurseries, Romsey, Hants
Notcutts, Woodbridge, Suffolk
Unusual plants (Beth Chatto), Elmstead Market,
Colchester, Essex.

CLAPHAM, TUTIN and WARBURG *Excursion Flora of the
British Isles,* Cambridge University Press

Hiller's Manual of Trees and Shrubs, David and Charles,
1981

Sanders' Encyclopaedia of Gardening, Hamlyn

ACKNOWLEDGMENTS

The publishers are grateful to the following for kindly
granting permission for their photographs to be included in
this book: Pat Brindley (pp 43, 62, 102); Peter McHoy (pp
47, 75, 79, 123); Photos Horticultural (pp 2/3, 4, 10, 11, 15,
19, 27, 35, 39, 50, 55, 59, 71, 91, 95, 98, 106, 107, 110, 114,
122) and Harry Smith (pp 83, 86, 115, 119).

All line drawings by John Woodcock

INDEX